FOLK ART

GIFTS FOR ALL SEASONS

FOLK ART

GIFTS FOR ALL SEASONS

Eva & Nicole Tummel

Kangaroo Press

To Susan, my dear god-daughter,
Nicole's cousin in Hungary.
With lots of love, Eva and Nicole

Front cover: *Small wooden trunk* (page 42)
and bottle stoppers (page 40) *feature in this*
assortment of collectibles.
Back cover: *Easter eggs* (page 110)

Tummel, Eva.
Folk art gifts for all seasons.

Includes index.
ISBN 0 86417 867 0.

1. Folk art. 2. Painting - Technique. 3. Gifts. I. Tummel, Nicole. II. Title.

745.72

First published in 1998 by Kangaroo Press Pty Ltd
An imprint of Simon & Schuster Australia
20 Barcoo Street (PO Box 507) East Roseville NSW 2069
Printed in Hong Kong by Colorcraft Ltd

Contents

Introduction

We have prepared this book in response to requests from many people over the last few years for gift ideas suitable for all ages.

There are over 100 projects, large and small, which make ideal everyday, Christmas and Easter gifts. Use your imagination to apply the patterns to other small shapes; for example, fridge magnets, mobiles, baskets and gift boxes, terracotta pots. There is nothing nicer than giving a gift to friends and family which you have painted yourself.

We hope you will enjoy painting these projects.

Happy painting!

Eva and Nicole

Materials

Paints

Waterbased acrylic paints (artist's colours). Make sure they are good quality. There are at least five different brands of paints presently on the market, some of better quality than others. I leave the choice to you, but please experiment to decide which brand you prefer to use. There are at least fifty to a hundred different colours available in most brands. You don't need to buy nearly that many, however; if you purchase the primary colours plus a few other colours, you will be able to mix at least another fifty shades or more.

Decorative colours come in 50 ml bottles or 75 ml tubes. Base coat colours come in 250 ml bottles or jars.

Varnishes

Waterbased polyurethane varnish (non-yellowing) is available in satin or gloss finish in 250 ml bottles. Use a soft fibre flat brush 12 mm or 25 mm (½" or 1") wide. Apply varnish with even strokes, in one direction only. Try not to go over the same strokes again. On most articles two coats of varnish are sufficient. You may wish to apply three or four coats for extra gloss and durability.

I have found from past experience that different batches of varnishes can vary quite a lot. I suggest you try them out first on a trial piece (something small), before you take the plunge and varnish your project.

Do read the instructions given on the bottles by the manufacturers. I normally leave my work for 24 hours before applying the first coat of varnish. Leave overnight to dry and then apply a second coat. Sand gently between coats.

Avoid varnishing in a draught or in front of a fan. Also try to avoid very humid or rainy days, as varnish tends to bubble under humid weather conditions.

Most varnishes have a slightly milky appearance when applied but a good varnish should dry to a clear finish. Always use a soft, good-quality brush for varnishing, otherwise the brush will create streakiness.

All purpose sealer

This is a very important medium that should be used in all base coat colours.

Some base coat paints already have sealer in them, so make sure you check this on the instruction label before adding sealer. Sealer also plays an important part in bonding the paint to the surface you are preparing to paint.

Flow medium

This medium makes your paint much easier to handle, because when it is added to paint it makes it flow nicely. Some brands already have flow medium in them, so check label before use. Mix one part flow medium to one part paint. Flow medium is very good to use in hot weather, or when you are painting curlicues. It is also helpful when doing lettering, and especially when painting long fine strokes, as it prevents the brush running out halfway through the stroke.

Crackling

When using crackle medium you must work fast, as crackle medium won't work after 24 hours. This means you must finish the project in one day.

1. After cleaning your article, paint with one coat of base coat colour mixed with sealer, and let dry. Next, apply in rapid succession four coats of base coat colour, this time paint only. Let dry between coats.
2. Trace design onto article and paint. Designs should be kept simple so you can paint them on in a short time.
3. As soon as design is dry, apply thick coat of crackle medium all over article.
4. Place in a warm area (under a desk light is ideal). Within 90 minutes small cracks will appear. Do not use a hairdryer to hasten the process.

Retarder and antiquing medium

A very useful medium in warm dry conditions, because it prolongs the drying time of the paints. When using this medium allow your project to dry for a longer period than usual before varnishing. Apply one coat of varnish and let it dry. Mix 1 part paint to 1 part retarder and antiquing medium. Brush this mixture gently onto your painted piece. Wipe back with a paper towel. If you wipe back straight away you will achieve a light antiquing. If you leave the mixture on for a longer period of time, you will achieve a darker effect. I feel this method should only be used on older pieces of furniture, as it looks out of character on newer items.

Essentials for beginners

Paints

At least 8 to 10 colours in waterbased acrylic paints (specially designed for folk art painting).

Brushes

4 basic brushes (good quality synthetic fibre), #00, #2, #4, #6 round, for painting designs.
1 flat brush 25 mm (1") wide, or #12 round brush.
1 flat brush 25 mm (1") wide for varnishing; must be soft fibre.

Varnish

1 bottle of polyurethane waterbased varnish. (Not household varnish.) Satin or gloss finish.

All purpose sealer

1 bottle

Palette

Round palette, 10 small dishes, a large dish in centre.

Wooden articles

Pine or plywood or craftwood.

For information on wooden articles and Country Folk Art Club membership write to Mrs Eva Tummel, 'Folklore House', PO Box 646, Nambour, Qld 4560.

Pencils

2B for drawing designs and tracing patterns.
5H for transferring design onto project.
White, black or peach colour carbon pencils for free-hand drawing.

Tracing paper, rubber & transfer paper

(black, white or yellow).

Sketch pad

For practice strokes and colour combinations; also use it for creating your own designs.

Sandpaper

Wet-and-dry #400 or #600

And

Water jar to rinse your brushes in.
Spray mist bottle to moisten the paint occasionally and prevent it from drying up.
Freezer bag to cover palette to preserve paint in between uses. Paints in palette will last for weeks if you look after them.

Finishes

Every project completed must have a good finish—without that your work is incomplete. Paint front, back, sides and *insides* of your projects! Varnish all your projects—it will protect them from dust and dirt, and highlight the paint colours.

Leftover paint

To store leftover or excess paint, use small airtight jars or plastic film canisters. Leftover paint can also be used for base-coating smaller articles—wooden spoons, small boxes, fridge magnets—or painting the insides of small boxes.

N.B. No responsibility is taken by the artists or the publishers of this book for any articles spoiled due to using inferior materials or not taking proper care!

Brushes and techniques

I recommend good quality synthetic fibre or synthetic sable brushes. (Pure sable brushes are not suitable for folk art painting or for use with acrylic paints.)

I use only round brushes for painting my designs, as the old traditional folk art was always done with round brushes. With round brushes you achieve a much softer effect. I use flat brushes only for base coating and varnishing.

The sizes we most often use are:

Round brushes #00, #2, #4, #6, #8.

Liner brush #1 to paint finer detailed work (for example, stems and curlicues).

Flat brush 25 mm (1") wide or #12 round brush for base coating.

Flat brush 25 mm (1") wide for varnishing, must be soft fibre.

Brush care

If quality brushes are properly cared for they will last for many years. Some of my brushes are over 30 years old and are still in perfect condition because of the way I have looked after them.

Loading of brushes

When you are loading your brush never let the paint reach the ferrule (metal part), as it will build up and dry inside the ferrule and split the fibres. Eventually the brushes will lose their points.

The paint should only be loaded halfway or at most three-quarters of the way up the fibre of the brush. Rinse frequently between strokes, and when you have finished painting make sure you rinse the brush thoroughly so that there is no paint left in the fibres.

Handy hint

We always tell our students to roll their brushes, once they are clean, over a cake of soap. Shape each brush to a point, then stand it upright in either a brush holder or a glass jar. This will keep the brushes in shape. The soap will dry but will not ruin your brush, and you can leave it in for any length of time. Before using again just rinse the soap out of the brush in cold water.

ROUND BRUSH TECHNIQUES

Comma stroke

The comma stroke is both the most important and the easiest stroke in folk art painting. Commas can look very effective as parts of different designs, and as fill-in strokes. When loading your brush for commas load it so it has a rounded head to begin the stroke.

To begin press down gently on the surface. Then gradually pull the brush towards you, releasing the pressure halfway through the stroke.

Make sure you come to a complete stop before lifting the brush off the surface. Do not flick the brush at the end of the stroke, as you will end up with a so-called 'fish tail', the result of losing control of the brush.

The S stroke

Start with the tip of the brush, and begin to pull it towards you, adding some pressure. Continue adding pressure as your stroke begins to go the other way, then gradually release the pressure. Finish the stroke by bringing the brush to a point, stopping and lifting the brush from the work. The most pressure should be applied in the middle part of the stroke.

Scroll or curlicue

With this stroke you can have a lot of fun. You can make the scrolls or curlicues curly, or make all sorts of patterns with them. Scrolls can be either thick or thin, depending on what sort of pressure you apply. You can achieve this stroke most easily with a liner brush, but you can also use a #00 round.

C stroke

To start this stroke begin with the tip of the brush. It must be perpendicular to the painting surface. Start pulling gently, then start to apply pressure gradually as you are entering the curved part of the stroke. This is the thickest part of the stroke. When leaving the centre of the curve start gently releasing pressure, and finish the stroke with a fine line.

Come to a complete stop and lift the brush off the surface.

Brush Strokes ~ Leaves
Double Loading Technique

Rose Bud Leaves

Strawberry

Violet Leaves

Roses

Trees

Cottage

Strawberry

Strawberry Flower

Tulip

Tulip leaves

Brush Strokes~Flowers
Double Loading Technique

Rose Buds

"Eva's Rose"

Violets

Forget-me-not

Traditional Rose

Daisies

Double Bow

Grapes

Pears

Apples

Project preparation

WOOD

Preparation before painting an article is very important in achieving a well finished product. These suggestions will help with different types of wooden surfaces.

New wood

Painted solid background colour.
1. Fill in cracks and holes with wood putty, let dry.
2. Sand with #400 wet and dry sandpaper.
3. Apply 1 coat of base coat colour with a 12 mm (½") flat brush. First coat: mix 1 part paint and 1 part sealer.
4. Let dry. Sand lightly, wipe off any dust with a lint-free cloth.
5. Apply second coat of base colour, let dry. Second coat: paint only.
6. Project is now ready to apply design and paint.

Old wood

Painted solid background colour.
1. Remove dust and dirt, grease marks and old polish. Clean surface with soapy water or sugar soap.
2. Fill in cracks and holes with wood putty, let dry.
3. Sand with #400 wet and dry sandpaper.
4. Apply 1 coat of base coat colour with 12 mm (½") flat brush. First coat: mix 1 part paint and 1 part sealer. Let dry. Sand lightly, wipe off any dust with a lint free cloth.
5. Apply second coat of base coat colour. Let dry. Second coat paint only!

Project is now ready to apply design and paint.

Natural wood

If you prefer to leave the timber a natural colour you must seal it with 1 coat of all purpose sealer, let it dry, then sand lightly before proceeding with painting.

Pre-painted wood

If the wooden article has been painted before, there is no need to strip back paint completely, just clean and sand well. Use the same method of preparation as for old wood above. Add sealer to first coat!

Second coat, paint only.

Project is now ready to apply design and paint.

Staining

Staining can look very effective, especially if you have a nice natural pine article. It really brings the grain out. Use any colour stain you wish, following this procedure:
1. Dampen your wooden article all over with a sponge. This is to prevent the stain soaking in too quickly or creating a blotchy or uneven colour.
2. Apply stain to one side only with a sponge or base coat brush. Wipe off excess paint with paper towel. Let dry.
3. Apply stain, one surface at a time, to sides and back of your article. Let dry. Before applying the design, sand gently with #400 sandpaper.

Stain recipe
   1 part paint
   1 part all purpose sealer
   1 part retarder
Depending on how deep you wish the stain to appear, add more or less water to the mixture.

Repeat staining procedure until you get to the desired shade. When dry the article is ready to be painted and varnished.

TIN

New tin

1. Clean well, sand lightly.
2. Paint with primer or spray with rustproofing solution. Let dry.

Your project is now ready for base coating.

Old tin

1. Clean well, using oven cleaner if necessary.
2. Remove rust by sanding or sandblasting.
3. Paint with primer or spray with rustproofing solution. Let dry. It is very important to remove all rust, as all waterbased acrylic paints will let rust through in time!

Your project is now ready for base coating.

TERRACOTTA

Use these techniques for preparing and base coating terracotta.

Terracotta (natural)

1. Clean terracotta thoroughly. If you use a damp cloth to remove dust and dirt, make sure you dry the article well before proceeding with painting.
2. Sand lightly with wet and dry sandpaper, wiping off any dust with a lint-free cloth.
3. Trace design from book onto tracing paper with 2B pencil.
4. Position design on terracotta item, placing white or black transfer paper between tracing paper and project.
5. Retrace design with 5H pencil. You might have to cut the pattern in half and trace one half first, then the other, as most items are rounded, making it hard to transfer designs. Try to freehand some of the designs.
6. Project is now ready to paint. Follow painting guide for each project.

Note:
1. You can paint straight onto terracotta.
2. You can paint terracotta with 1 coat of all purpose sealer before painting.
3. You can add a few drops of sealer to each colour.

Terracotta (coloured background)

Base coat
First coat: 1 part paint + 1 part all purpose sealer.
Second coat: Paint only!

1. Clean terracotta article thoroughly. If you use a damp cloth to remove dust and dirt, dry the article well before applying base coat colour.
2. Sand lightly with wet and dry sandpaper, wiping off any dust with a lint-free cloth.
3. Apply first coat of base coat colour mixed with all purpose sealer using 12 mm (½") flat brush or #12 round brush. Let dry well before applying second coat of colour.
4. Paint second coat of base coat colour, this time paint only. (If a third coat is necessary for better coverage apply paint only.)
5. Trace design from book onto tracing paper with 2B pencil.
6. Position design on terracotta item, placing white or black transfer paper between tracing paper and project.
7. Retrace design with 2H pencil. Try to freehand some of the design.

Project is now ready to paint. Follow painting guide for each project.

BASE COATING

Base coating is a very important part of preparing your project, and of achieving a well finished article.
    You have two choices with base coat paints:

1. Base coat paint without added all purpose sealer. In this case you must mix 1 part paint to 1 part all purpose sealer. Paint first coat with mixture, second coat apply paint only.
2. Base coat paint with all purpose sealer already added. In this case just apply two coats of paint. Make sure you sand between coats.
3. Another option which you might like to experiment with is: Apply just straight all purpose sealer to your project. Then proceed with 1 coat of all purpose sealer plus paint. Follow this with 1 coat of paint only. Remember it is a must to sand between each coat to get a nice smooth finish.

With most colours 2 coats are sufficient. Some of the lighter or more transparent colours in certain brands may require 3 or 4 coats for good coverage.

In most brands of waterbased acrylic artist's colours formulated especially for folk art painting you will find a large range of base coat colours which come in 250 ml bottles or jars.

Use these for base coating, as it is more economical. Use the tubes, which are more expensive, for your leaves and flowers only.

Please do not use ordinary household paints for base coating, as most are toxic and will not give the same finish. It is also dangerous to mix different types of paints because a chemical reaction can occur. For example, your design can peel off or come off while varnishing. Most of all, though, such reactions can be extremely dangerous for people who suffer from serious allergies.

MARBLING

To create this effect you apply 2 contrasting layers of paint. When you are applying the second layer, use a wider brush and gently swirl at random through the colours. Next take a feather and, using the tip, drag it through the paint to get the marbled effect. Marbling is mostly used on larger pieces, for example, on the sides of a cabinet or wardrobe. You never paint a design over areas which have been marbled.

SPONGING

This gives a nice effect, especially when used on terracotta. Like marbling, you apply 2 contrasting layers of paint. Allow the first colour to dry completely before applying second colour. While the second colour is still wet, dab a sponge over the surface. It's as easy as that.

THE PROJECTS

Large grey coathanger

Illustrated on page 22

Materials

Large pine coathanger
Paints: Waterbased acrylics
Brushes: #4, #2, #00 round brushes; 12 mm and 25 mm (½" and 1") flat brushes
Tracing paper, black transfer paper
Varnish: Polyurethane satin finish
Pencils: 2B and 5H
Sandpaper: Wet-and-dry #400 and #600

Palette

Base coat: Grey
Leaves: Dark green + white
Flowers: Red + white + blue
Birds: Blue + yellow + red + orange + white
Dots: White + yellow

Preparation

1. Apply 1 coat of base coat colour to coathanger with 12 mm (½") flat brush.
2. Let dry. Sand lightly, apply second coat of base coat colour. Let dry.
3. Trace design onto tracing paper.
4. Place pattern onto article, slide the black transfer paper between tracing paper and article.
5. Retrace design with 5H pencil.

Painting guide

1. Leaves: Double load #2 brush with dark green and white, paint all leaves and stems.
2. Flowers: With #2 brush paint all petals red and white. Centres of flowers are painted blue. Lines and dots in centre of flower are painted white with #00 brush.
3. Birds: Bodies and heads are painted solid blue using #4 brush. Part of wing is painted orange and white, double loaded, with #4 brush. Top and bottom parts of wings are painted solid yellow with #2 brush; as is the beak. Tail is painted solid red with #4 brush. Red and blue dots in wings are painted with #00 brush. Eyes—large white dot with small blue dot in the middle, using #00 brush.
4. Dots: Paint white and yellow with #00 brush.

Finish

Apply 1 coat of satin finish polyurethane varnish with 25 mm (1") flat brush. Let dry overnight. Then apply a second coat of varnish. Sand gently between coats.

centre, fold

Large black coathanger

Illustrated on page 22

Materials

Large wooden coathanger
Paints: Waterbased acrylics
Brushes: #6, #4, #2, #00 round brushes; 12 mm
   and 25 mm (½" and 1") flat brushes
Tracing paper, white transfer paper
Varnish: Polyurethane satin finish
Pencils: 2B and 5H
Sandpaper: Wet-and-dry #400 and #600

Palette

Base coat: Black
Leaves: Green + white
Roses: Red + white
Tulip: Blue + white
Flowers: Orange + blue + white
Curlicues: Gold

Preparation

1. Apply 1 coat of base coat colour to coathanger
   with 12 mm (½") flat brush.
2. Let dry. Sand lightly, apply second coat of base
   coat colour. Let dry.
3. Trace design onto tracing paper.
4. Place pattern onto coathanger; slide white transfer paper between tracing paper and coathanger.
5. Retrace design with 5H pencil.

Painting guide

1. Leaves: Double load #6 brush with green and
   white; paint all large leaves. Smaller leaves are
   painted with #2 brush.
2. Roses: Double load red and white and paint roses
   with #4 brush. Centres are painted solid red; white
   dots in centre are painted with #00 brush.
3. Tulip: Paint petals with #6 brush, double loading
   with blue and white.
4. Flowers: Using #4 brush paint all petals orange
   and white. Centres are painted solid blue with #2
   brush. White dots in centres of flowers: paint with
   #00 brush.
5. Curlicues: Paint solid gold with #00 brush.

Finish

Apply 1 coat of satin finish polyurethane varnish with
25 mm (1") flat brush. Let this dry overnight. Apply a
second coat of varnish. Sand gently between coats.

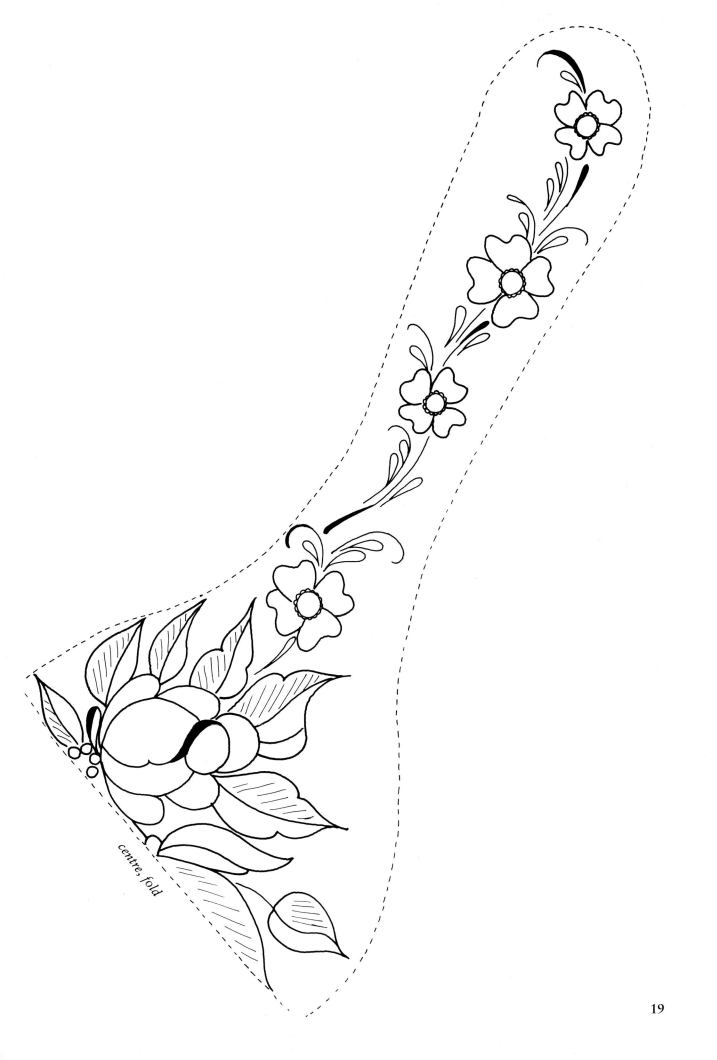

centre, fold

19

Slim coathanger

Illustrated on page 22

Materials

Pine coathanger
Paints: Waterbased acrylics
Brushes: #4, #2, #00 round brushes; 12 mm and 25 mm (½" and 1") flat brushes
Tracing paper, black transfer paper
Varnish: Polyurethane satin finish
Pencils: 2B and 5H
Sandpaper: Wet-and-dry #400 or #600

Palette

Base coat: Cream
Leaves: Green + white
Roses: Pink + white
Small flowers: Blue + white + yellow
Commas: Gold

Preparation

1. Apply 1 coat of base coat colour to coathanger with 12 mm (½") flat brush.
2. Let dry. Sand lightly, apply second coat of base coat colour. Let dry.
3. Trace design onto tracing paper.
4. Place pattern onto article, slide the black transfer paper between tracing paper and article.
5. Retrace design with 5H pencil.

Painting guide

1. Leaves: Double load #4 brush with green and white, paint all leaves.
2. Roses: Paint roses pink first with #4 brush. Then double load pink and white, and paint all petals with #2 brush. Bottom petals should be outlined only. White dots in centre are painted with #00 brush.
3. Small flowers: Double load #2 brush with blue and white; paint all petals. Centres are painted yellow and white using same brush.
4. Commas: Paint solid gold using #2 brush.

Finish

Apply 1 coat of satin finish polyurethane varnish with 25 mm (1") flat brush. Let dry overnight. Apply a second coat of varnish. Sand gently between coats.

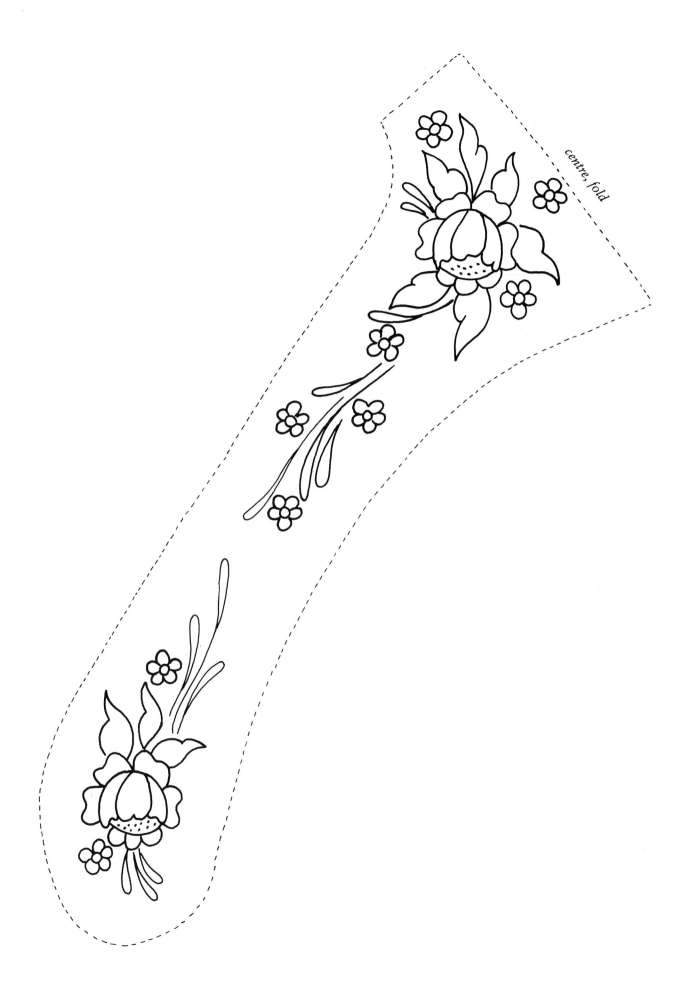

centre fold

21

Coathangers
(see pages 16–21)

22

Small ballet case
(see page 24)

23

Small ballet case

Illustrated on page 23

Materials

Pine ballet case
Paints: Waterbased acrylics
Brushes: #4, #2, #00 round brushes; 12 mm and
   25 mm (½" and 1") flat brushes
Tracing paper, black transfer paper
Varnish: Polyurethane satin finish
Pencils: 2B and 5H
Sandpaper: Wet-and-dry #400 or #600

Palette

Base coat: Pink
Leaves: Green + white
Hearts: Dark pink + white
Dot flowers: White
Bears: Light brown + dark brown + white + black
Bows: Blue + white + pink

Preparation

1. Apply 1 coat of base coat colour to ballet case with
   12 mm (½") flat brush.
2. Let dry. Sand lightly, apply second coat of base
   coat colour. Let dry.
3. Trace design onto tracing paper.
4. Place pattern onto ballet case; slide black transfer
   paper between tracing paper and ballet case.
5. Retrace design with 5H pencil.

Painting guide

1. Leaves: Double load green and white and paint
   all leaves with #2 brush.
2. Hearts: Paint with #2 brush pink and white.
3. Dot flowers: Paint white with #00 brush.
4. Bears: Paint bears dark brown first with #4 brush.
   Then with #2 brush paint pads, nose parts and
   inner ears lighter brown. Double load #2 brush
   with light brown and white. Paint over dark part
   of bears with a dry brush effect. Paint eyes and
   noses black with #00 brush. Paint white on eyes
   and noses using #00 brush.
5. Bows: Paint with #2 brush: double load blue and
   white for one bear; for the other bear double load
   pink and white.

Finish

Apply 1 coat of satin finish polyurethane varnish with
25 mm (1") flat brush. Let it dry overnight. Apply a
second coat of varnish. Sand gently between coats.

Small ducks with golden beaks

Illustrated on page 30

Materials

Three terracotta ducks
Paints: Waterbased acrylics
Brushes: #2, #00 round brushes; 12 mm and 25 mm
   (½" and 1") flat brushes
Tracing paper, black transfer paper
Varnish: Polyurethane satin finish
Pencils: 2B and 5H
Sandpaper: Wet-and-dry #400 or #600

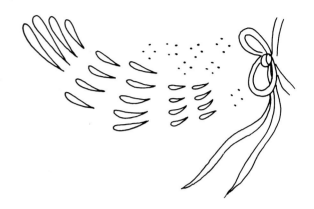

Palette

Base coat: White
Leaves: Green + white
Forget-me-nots: Blue + white + yellow
Small flowers: Blue + pink
Bows: Blue + pink + white
Eyes: Dark brown
Cheeks: Soft pink
Beaks: Green, dark brown
Feathers: Light blue + grey + white

Preparation

1. Apply 1 coat of base coat colour to each duck with
   12 mm (½") flat brush.
2. Let dry. Sand lightly, apply second coat of base
   coat colour. Let dry.
3. Trace design onto tracing paper.
4. Place pattern onto duck, slide the black transfer
   paper between tracing paper and duck.
5. Retrace design with 5H pencil.

Painting guide

Duck 1

1. Leaves: Double load green and white using #2
   brush.
2. Forget-me-nots: Using #2 brush double load blue
   and white and paint all petals. Paint the centres
   yellow and white using same brush.
3. Beak: Paint green.

Ducks 2 & 3

1. Small flowers: Using #00 brush paint blue dots
   on one duck and pink dots on the other duck.
2. Beaks: Paint dark brown.

All ducks

1. Bows: Double load blue and white or pink and
   white and paint bows with #2 brush.
2. Eyes: With #00 brush paint eyes solid brown.
3. Cheeks: Using a stippled brush effect paint cheeks
   light pink with #00 brush.
4. Feathers: Triple load blue, grey and white and
   paint all feathers with #2 brush.

Finish

Apply 1 coat of satin finish polyurethane varnish with
25 mm (1") flat brush.
Let dry overnight. Apply second coat of varnish.

Glass serviette holder

Illustrated on page 30

Materials

Glass serviette holder
Paints: Waterbased acrylics
Brushes: #2, #00 round brushes; 12 mm and 25 mm
  (½" and 1") flat brushes
Tracing paper, black transfer paper
Varnish: Polyurethane gloss finish
Pencils: 2B, 5H

Palette

Base coat duck: White
Bow: Blue
Beak, feet: Yellow
Eyes: Black
Flowers: White
Centre: Yellow
Stems: Green

Preparation

1. Apply 1 coat of all purpose sealer to areas you are painting. Let dry.
2. Trace design onto tracing paper.
3. Place pattern onto serviette holder, slide black transfer paper between tracing paper and glass.
4. Retrace design with 5H pencil.

Painting guide

1. Duck: Using #2 brush paint whole duck solid white.
2. Bow: Paint bow solid blue using same brush.
3. Beak, feet: With #00 brush paint feet and beak solid yellow.
4. Eyes: Using #00 brush paint eyes black.
5. Flowers: With #2 brush paint all petals solid white.
6. Centre: Paint centres yellow using #00 brush.
7. Stems: Using green paint all stems with #00 brush.

Finish

Apply 1 coat of gloss finish polyurethane varnish with 25 mm (1") flat brush. Let dry overnight. Apply a second coat of varnish.

Small clog

Illustrated on page 31

Materials

Terracotta clog
Paints: Waterbased acrylics
Brushes: #2, #1, #00 round brushes; 12 mm and
25 mm (½" and 1") flat brushes
Tracing paper, white transfer paper
Varnish: Polyurethane gloss finish
Pencils: 2B and 5H
Sandpaper: Wet-and-dry #400 or #600

Palette

Base coat: Deep blue
Leaves: Antique green + white
Commas: Deep green + white
Flowers: Blue + yellow + red + brown + white
Small flowers: Yellow + brown

Preparation

1. Apply 1 coat of base coat colour to clog with
   12 mm (½") flat brush.
2. Let dry. Sand lightly, apply second coat of base
   coat colour. Let dry.
3. Trace design onto tracing paper.
4. Place pattern onto clog, slide white transfer paper
   between tracing paper and clog.
5. Retrace design with 5H pencil.

Painting guide

1. Leaves: Double load #2 brush with antique green
   and white, and paint large leaves.
2. Commas: With #2 brush paint all commas,
   double loading deep green and white. Small
   antique green leaves and stems: double load with
   white using #1 brush.
3. Flowers: Using #2 brush paint 3 different centre
   flowers, double loading red, blue, and yellow with
   white. Centres paint solid brown with #2 brush.
4. Small flowers: Paint solid yellow dots using #00
   brush; paint centres brown with same brush.

Finish

Apply 1 coat of gloss finish polyurethane varnish with
25 mm (1") flat brush. Let dry overnight. Apply a
second coat of varnish. Sand gently between coats.

Medium clog

Illustrated on page 31

Materials

Terracotta clog
Paints: Waterbased acrylics
Brushes: #4, #2, #00 round brushes; 12 mm and
  25 mm (½" and 1") flat brushes
Tracing paper, white transfer paper
Varnish: Polyurethane gloss finish
Pencils: 2B and 5H
Sandpaper: Wet-and-dry #400 or #600

Palette

Base coat: Deep blue
Leaves: Deep green + white
Tulips: Red + blue + white
Centre flower: Light blue + green + white
Other flowers: Yellow + brown
Small flowers: White
Heart: Red

Preparation

1. Apply 1 coat of base coat colour to clog with
   12 mm (½") flat brush.
2. Let dry. Sand lightly, apply second coat of base
   coat colour. Let dry.
3. Trace design onto tracing paper.
4. Place pattern onto clog, slide white transfer paper
   between tracing paper and clog.
5. Retrace design with 5H pencil.

Painting guide

1. Leaves: Double load #2 brush with deep green
   and white and paint all leaves.
2. Tulips: With #4 brush double load red and white,
   or blue and white, and paint all tulips. Using #2
   brush paint light blue comma in centre of each
   tulip. Outline with white dots using #00 brush.
3. Centre flower: Double load blue and white with
   #2 brush and paint all petals. Paint green dot in
   centre using same brush. Small white dots are
   painted white using #00 brush.
4. Yellow flowers: Paint solid yellow using #2 brush.
   Paint centres brown using same brush.
5. Small flowers: Using #00 brush paint the small
   flowers and dots solid white.

6. Heart: Paint solid red using #4 brush. You may
   need 3 coats.

Finish

Apply 1 coat of gloss finish polyurethane varnish with
25 mm (1") flat brush. Let dry overnight. Apply a
second coat of varnish. Sand gently between coats.

front

back

*Small ducks with golden beaks
and glass serviette holder
(see pages 26 and 27)*

30

Clogs
(see pages 28–29 and 32)

Large clog

Illustrated on page 31

Materials

Pair of large terracotta clogs
Paints: Waterbased acrylics
Brushes: #4, #2, #00 round brushes; 12 mm and
25 mm (½" and 1") flat brushes
Tracing paper, white transfer paper
Varnish: Polyurethane gloss finish
Pencils: 2B and 5H
Sandpaper: Wet-and-dry #400 or #600

Palette

Base coat: Blue
Commas: Green + white
Tulips: Red + blue
+ yellow + white
Heart: Red
Stems: Green + white
Figures
Pants, skirt, hat: Black
+ white
Blouses, apron, girl's hat:
Light blue + white
Vests: Red
Buttons: White
Faces: Flesh colour
Hair: Yellow + white

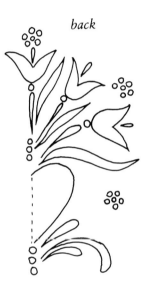

back

side

Preparation

1. Apply 1 coat of base coat colour to
clogs with 12 mm (½") flat brush.
2. Let dry. Sand lightly, apply second
coat of base coat colour. Let dry.
3. Trace design onto tracing paper.
4. Place pattern onto clog, slide white
transfer paper between the tracing
paper and clog.
5. Retrace design with 5H pencil.

Painting guide

1. Commas: With #00 brush double load green and
white.
2. Tulips: Follow page 31 for different colours; with
#4 and #2 brushes paint all tulips solid colours.

3. Heart: With #4 brush paint heart solid red.
4. Stems: Using #00 brush double load green and
white and paint all stems.
5. Pants, skirt, hat: Double load #2 brush with black
and white.
6. Blouses, apron, hat: Using #2 brush double load
light blue and white.
7. Vests: Paint solid red using #2 brush.
8. Buttons: With #00 brush paint solid white.
9. Face: Paint flesh colour with #2 brush. Eyes blue
using #00 brush. Mouth red, and cheeks light pink,
using dry brush effect.
10. Hair: Using #2 brush double load yellow and
white.

Finish

Apply 1 coat of gloss finish polyurethane varnish with
25 mm (1") flat brush. Let dry overnight. Apply a
second coat of varnish. Sand gently between coats.

front

Doll's house furniture

Illustrated on page 38

Materials

Wooden doll's house furniture
Paints: Waterbased acrylics
Brushes: #4, #2, #00 round brushes; 12 mm and 25 mm (½" and 1") flat brushes
Tracing paper, white transfer paper
Varnish: Polyurethane gloss finish
Pencils: 2B and 5H
Sandpaper: Wet-and-dry #400 or #600

Palette

Base coat: Antique blue
Leaves: Mid green + white
Stems: Mid green + white
Heart: Deep red
Tulip: Blue + white
Daisies: White + brown + yellow
Stamens: Brown + white
Small flower: Blue + white + yellow

Preparation

1. Apply 1 coat of base coat colour to all pieces of furniture with 12 mm (½") flat brush.
2. Let dry. Sand lightly, apply second coat of base coat colour. Let dry.
3. Trace design onto tracing paper.
4. Place pattern onto article, slide the white transfer paper between tracing paper and article.
5. Retrace design with 5H pencil.

Painting guide

1. Leaves: Double load #2 brush with green and white and paint all leaves. Use same technique for stems but use a #00 brush.
2. Heart: With #4 brush paint all hearts solid red. You will need to do a few coats.
3. Tulips: Double load blue and white and paint all tulips with #2 brush.
4. Daisies: Paint solid white using #4 brush. When dry paint stamens brown with #00 brush and add white dots on the ends.
5. Small flowers: Double load blue and white with #2 brush. With same brush double load yellow and white and paint centres.

Finish

Apply 1 coat of gloss finish polyurethane varnish with 25 mm (1") flat brush. Let dry overnight. Apply a second coat of varnish. Sand gently between coats.

Kitchen chair—back

Kitchen chair—seat

Kitchen table

centre

Bench seat—back

Bench seat—seat

Bench seat— front

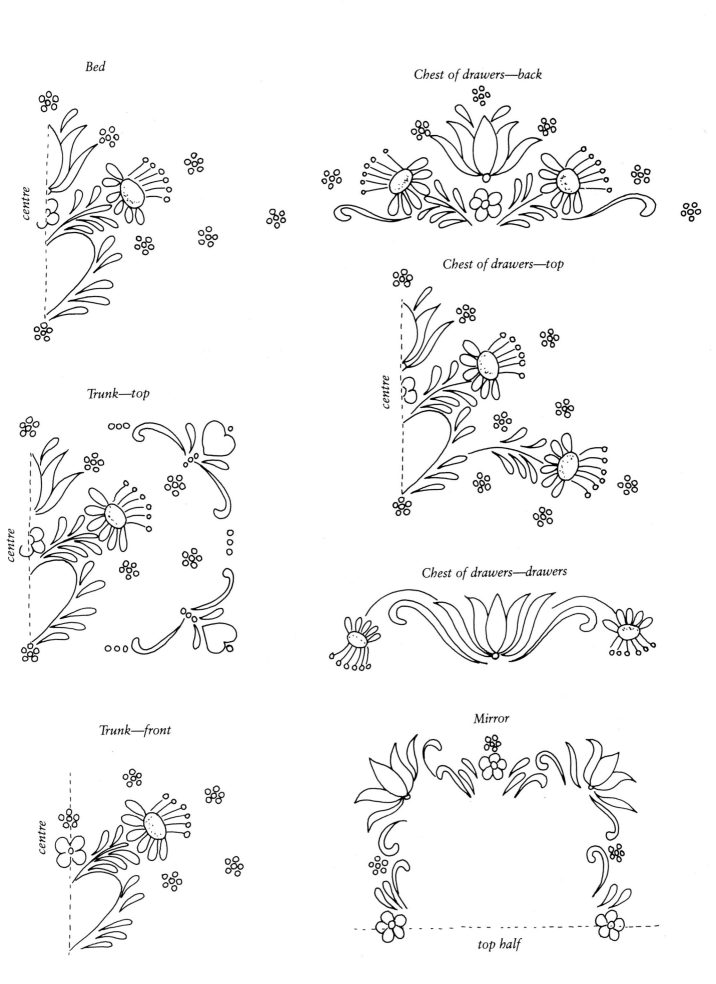

Bed

Chest of drawers—back

Chest of drawers—top

Trunk—top

centre

centre

Chest of drawers—drawers

Trunk—front

centre

Mirror

top half

35

Pencil box

Illustrated on page 39

Materials

Wooden pencil box
Paints: Waterbased acrylics
Brushes: #4, #2, #00 round brushes; 12 mm and
    25 mm (½" and 1") flat brushes
Tracing paper, white transfer paper
Varnish: Polyurethane gloss varnish
Pencils: 2B and 5H
Sandpaper: Wet-and-dry #400 or #600

Palette

Base coat: Black + red
Leaves: Dark green
Tulip 1: Yellow + blue + red + white
Tulip 2: Yellow + blue + red + pink
Tulip 3: Yellow + blue + red
Flower: Yellow + pink + blue + red
Dots: White
Curlicues: Gold

Preparation

1. Apply 1 coat of base coat colour to pencil box with 12 mm (½") flat brush.
2. Let dry. Sand lightly, apply second coat of base coat colour. Let dry.
3. Trace design onto tracing paper.
4. Place pattern onto box, slide white transfer paper between tracing paper and box.
5. Retrace design with 5H pencil.

Painting guide

1. Leaves: Paint all leaves dark green with #2 brush.
2. Tulip 1: Paint centre of flower yellow with #4 brush. Using #00 brush paint criss-cross lines white. Blue tulip petals, plus scallops on bottom, are painted solid blue with #4 brush. Red petals: paint with #2 brush.
3. Tulip 2: With #4 brush paint centre yellow. Using #2 brush paint red petals solid red. Pink petals are painted with #2 brush. Blue petals plus centre comma are painted solid blue with #2 brush.
4. Tulip 3: Paint centre yellow with #4 brush. Outer petals paint red using same brush. Centre is painted blue with #2 brush.
5. Flower: Paint pink part of flower first with #2 brush. Centre is painted yellow using same brush. Blue line around flower is painted with #00 brush. Red dots in centre of flowers are painted with #00 brush.
6. Dots: All dots painted white using #00 brush.
7. Curlicues: Paint gold with #00 brush.

Finish

Apply 1 coat of gloss finish polyurethane varnish with 25 mm (1") flat brush. Let dry overnight. Apply a second coat of varnish. Sand gently between coats.

Doll's house furniture
(see pages 33–35)

Pencil box and small trunk
(see pages 36 and 42)

black

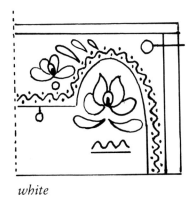

white

yellow

cream

Bottle stoppers

Black and white stoppers illustrated on the front cover

Materials

4 wooden cork stoppers
Paints: Waterbased acrylics
Brushes: #2, #4, #00 round brushes
Tracing paper, white transfer paper
Varnish: Polyurethane gloss finish
Pencils: 2B and 5H
Sandpaper: Wet-and-dry #400 or #600

Preparation

1. Apply 1 coat of base coat colour to cork stopper with 12 mm (½") flat brush.
2. Let dry. Sand lightly, apply second coat of base coat colour. Let dry.
3. Trace design onto tracing paper.
4. Place pattern onto stopper, slide white transfer paper between tracing paper and stopper.
5. Retrace design with 5H pencil.

Painting guide (for all four stoppers)

1. The diagrams shown are only half of the pattern; to complete the project, repeat the design. When painting is complete, glue the cork onto the base.
2. Paint jackets on figures with #4 brush.
3. Paint face, hair and hat using #2 brush .
4. Eyes, moustache: Paint black with #00 brush.
5. Flowers: Use #2 brush for larger petals and #00 brush for smaller flowers and leaves.
6. Dots: Paint with #00 brush.

1. White stopper
Palette

Base coat: White
Face: Flesh colour
Hair: Brown
Hat: Black
Eyes, moustache: Black
Outline of jacket: Black
Flowers: Pink and red
Centre: Yellow and blue
Commas: Green
Zigzag: Yellow
Solid line: Red

2. Black stopper
Palette

Base coat: Black
Face: Flesh colour
Hair: Brown
Hat: Black
Eyes, moustache: Black
Outline of jacket: White
Flowers: Pink
Centre: Yellow and blue
Commas: Turquoise
Zigzag: Yellow
Solid line: Red

3. Yellow stopper
Palette

Base coat: Yellow
Face: Flesh colour
Hair: Brown
Hat: Black
Eyes, moustache: Black
Outline of jacket: Dark blue
Tulip: Mid blue
Dotts/dot flowers: White
Leaves: Dark green

4. Cream stopper
Palette

Base coat: Cream
Face: Flesh colour
Hair: Black
Hat: Brown
Eyes, moustache: Black
Outline of jacket: Red
Roses: Red
Small flowers: Blue, centre yellow
Leaves: Green

Finish

Apply 1 coat of gloss finish polyurethane varnish; use 25 mm (1") flat brush. Let dry, preferably overnight. Apply second coat of varnish, sand gently between coats.

Small trunk

Illustrated on page 39

Materials

Small wooden trunk
Paints: Waterbased acrylics
Brushes: #2, #00 round brushes; 12 mm and 25 mm
  (½" and 1") flat brushes
Tracing paper, white transfer paper
Varnish: Polyurethane gloss finish
Pencils: 2B and 5H
Sandpaper: Wet-and-dry #400 or #600

Palette

Base coat: Wood stain
Leaves: Dark green + light green
Tulips: Red + yellow
Flower: Dark blue + light blue
Round buds: Red + dark blue
Dots: Soft pink
Forget-me-nots: Blue + yellow
Border: Brown

Preparation

1. Apply wood stain to box. Let dry.
2. Trace design onto tracing paper.
3. Place pattern onto box, slide white transfer paper
   between tracing paper and box.
4. Retrace design with 5H pencil.

Painting guide

1. Leaves: With #00 brush paint leaves solid dark
   green and solid light green following photograph.
2. Tulips: Using #2 brush paint tulips solid red. Then
   add solid yellow using #00 brush.
3. Flower: First paint dark blue part of flower with
   #2 brush. Then add the light blue to rest of flower
   using same brush.
4. Round buds: With #2 brush paint first part of
   bud solid red. When dry add dark blue to top of
   bud using #00 brush.
5. Dots: Paint soft pink using #00 brush.
6. Forget-me-nots: Paint flower solid blue with #00
   brush. Paint centres yellow using same brush.
7. Borders: Paint brown using #00 brush.

Finish

Apply 1 coat of gloss finish polyurethane varnish with
25 mm (1") flat brush. Let dry, preferably overnight.
Apply a second coat of varnish.

Small watering can

Illustrated on page 46

Materials

Tin watering can
Paints: Waterbased acrylics
Brushes: #2, #00 round brushes; 12 mm and 25 mm
  (½" and 1") flat brushes
Tracing paper, white transfer paper
Varnish: Polyurethane satin finish
Pencils: 2B and 5H
Sandpaper: Wet-and-dry #400 or #600

Palette

Base coat: Burgundy
Leaves: Green
Flowers: White + yellow
Snall dotted lines: Gold

Preparation

1. Apply 1 coat of base coat colour to watering can
   with 12 mm (½") flat brush.
2. Let dry. Sand lightly, apply second coat of base
   coat colour. Let dry.
3. Trace design onto tracing paper.
4. Place pattern onto watering can, slide white transfer paper between tracing paper and can.
5. Retrace design with 5H pencil.

Painting guide

1. Leaves: Paint all leaves solid green with #00 brush.
2. Flowers: Using #2 brush paint all petals white,
   centres are painted yellow.
3. Lines: Paint gold using #00 brush.
4. Edges and handles: Paint solid gold.

Finish

Apply 1 coat of satin finish polyurethane varnish with
25 mm (1") flat brush. Let dry overnight. Apply a
second coat of varnish. Sand gently between coats.

Small bucket

Illustrated on page 46

Materials

Small metal bucket
Paints: Waterbased acrylics
Brushes: #2, #00 round brushes; 12 mm and 25 mm
   (½" and 1") flat brushes
Tracing paper, white transfer paper
Varnish: Polyurethane satin finish
Pencils: 2B and 5H
Sandpaper: Wet-and-dry #400 or #600

Palette

Base coat: Burgundy
Leaves: Pale green + white
Star flowers: Pale blue + white + green
Mauve flowers: Mauve + white + yellow
Edges: Gold

Preparation

1. Apply 1 coat of base coat colour to bucket with
   12 mm (½") flat brush.
2. Let dry. Sand lightly, apply second coat of base
   coat colour. Let dry.
3. Trace design onto tracing paper.
4. Place pattern on bucket, slide the white transfer
   paper between tracing paper and bucket.
5. Retrace design with 5H pencil.

Painting guide

1. Leaves: Paint all leaves pale green and white, double loading #2 brush.
2. Star flowers: Double load pale blue with white,
   paint all petals with #2 brush. Centres are painted
   green and white with #00 brush.
3. Mauve flowers: Paint centre of flower solid mauve
   with #2 brush. For petals double load mauve with
   white. In centre of flower add yellow and white
   commas with #00 brush.
4. Edges: Paint solid gold with #2 brush.

Finish

Apply 1 coat of satin finish polyurethane varnish with
25 mm (1") flat brush. Let this dry overnight. Apply a
second coat of varnish. Sand gently between coats.

Metal tub

Illustrated on page 46

Materials

Small metal tub
Paints: Waterbased acrylics
Brushes: #2, #00 round brushes; 12 mm and 25 mm
  (½" and 1") flat brushes
Tracing paper, white transfer paper
Varnish: Polyurethane satin finish
Pencils: 2B and 5H
Sandpaper: Wet-and-dry #400 or #600

Palette

Base coat: Burgundy
Leaves: Green + white + brown
Flowers: Pale pink + white + green + red
Dots: Gold

Preparation

1. Apply 1 coat of base coat colour to the tub with
   12 mm (½") flat brush.
2. Let dry. Sand lightly, apply second coat of base coat
   colour. Let dry.
3. Trace design onto tracing paper.
4. Place pattern onto tub, slide white transfer paper
   between tracing paper and tub.
5. Retrace design with 5H pencil.

Painting guide

1. Leaves: Double load green and white with #00
   brush; stems are painted brown and white.
2. Flowers: Double load #2 brush with pink and
   white and paint all petals. Centres are painted
   green, white dots are painted with #00 brush; add
   a touch of burgundy to centre.
3. Dots: Paint gold with #00 brush. Paint edges and
   scallops solid gold, using #2 brush.

Finish

Apply 1 coat of satin finish polyurethane varnish with
25 mm (1") flat brush. Let dry overnight. Apply a
second coat of varnish. Sand gently between coats.

Burgundy tin set and paper fan
(see pages 43, 44, 45, 48 and 52)

Black tin set
(see pages 49, 50 and 51)

47

Pitcher

Illustrated on page 46

Materials

Small metal pitcher
Paints: Waterbased acrylics
Brushes: #2, #00 round brushes; 12 mm and 25 mm
  (½" and 1") flat brushes
Tracing paper, white transfer paper
Varnish: Polyurethane satin finish
Pencils: 2B and 5H
Sandpaper: Wet-and-dry #400 or #600

Palette

Base coat: Burgundy
Leaves: Green + white + gold
Large flowers: Blue + yellow + white
Small flowers, buds: Pale blue + white
Stems: Brown + white

Preparation

1. Apply 1 coat of base coat colour to pitcher with
   12 mm (½") flat brush.
2. Let dry. Sand lightly, apply second coat of base
   coat colour. Let dry.
3. Trace design onto tracing paper.
4. Place pattern onto pitcher, slide the white transfer
   paper between tracing paper and pitcher.
5. Retrace design with 5H pencil.

Painting guide

1. Leaves: Double load #2 brush with green and
   white; paint all leaves.
2. Large flowers: Paint petals solid blue with #2
   brush. Dark blue lines are painted with #00 brush.
   Lines in centre of flowers are painted yellow, dots
   white with #00 brush.
3. Small flowers and buds: Paint flowers and buds
   pale blue first, then double load pale blue and white
   and paint all petals with #2 brush.
4. Stems: Paint brown and white stems for the blue
   flowers, and green stems for the lighter coloured
   flowers. Add some gold leaves here and there.
5. Handles and edges: Paint solid gold.

Finish

Apply 1 coat of satin finish polyurethane varnish with
25 mm (1") flat brush. Let dry overnight. Apply a
second coat of varnish. Sand gently between coats.

Two tubs

Illustrated on page 47

Materials

Two metal tubs
Paints: Waterbased acrylics
Brushes: #2, #00 round brushes; 12 mm and 25 mm
 (½" and 1") flat brushes
Tracing paper, white transfer paper
Varnish: Polyurethane gloss finish
Pencils: 2B and 5H
Sandpaper: Wet-and-dry #400 or #600

Palette

Base coat: Black
Leaves: Green + white
Roses: Red + white
Hearts: Red
Forget-me-nots: Blue + white + yellow
Dots: White
Lattice work: White
Edges: Gold

Preparation

1. Apply 1 coat of base coat colour to the tubs with
   12 mm (½") flat brush.
2. Let dry. Sand lightly, apply second coat of base
   coat colour. Let dry.
3. Trace design onto tracing paper.
4. Place pattern onto tub, slide white transfer paper
   between tracing paper and tub.
5. Retrace design with 5H pencil.

Painting guide

1. Leaves: Paint all leaves and comma strokes with
   #2 brush. Double load with green and white.
2. Roses: Paint half of circle solid red, the other half
   white, with #2 brush, and twirl one colour into
   the other with end of brush.
3. Hearts: Paint solid red with #2 brush.
4. Forget-me-nots: Double load blue and white
   using #2 brush. Using same brush paint centres
   yellow and white.
5. Dots: With #00 brush paint all dots white.
6. Lattice work: Paint white with #00 brush. Dotted lines to be painted gold.
7. Edges, handles: Paint solid gold with #2 brush.

Finish

Apply 1 coat of gloss finish polyurethane varnish with
25 mm (1") flat brush. Let dry overnight. Apply a
second coat of varnish. Sand gently between coats.

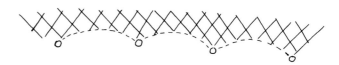

Small frying pan & bucket

Illustrated on page 47

Materials

Small tin frying pan and bucket
Paints: Waterbased acrylics
Brushes: #2, #00 round brushes; 12 mm and 25 mm
  (½" and 1") flat brushes
Tracing paper, white transfer paper
Varnish: Polyurethane gloss finish
Pencils: 2B and 5H
Sandpaper: Wet-and-dry #400 or #600

Palette

Base coat: Black
Leaves: Green + white
Roses: Red + white
Forget-me-nots: Blue + white + yellow
Commas: Green + white
Edge: Gold

Preparation

1. Apply 1 coat of base coat colour to each article
   with 12 mm (½") flat brush.
2. Let dry. Sand lightly, apply second coat of base
   coat colour. Let dry.
3. Trace design onto tracing paper.
4. Place patterns onto articles and slide white transfer paper between tracing paper and articles.
5. Retrace design with 5H pencil.

Painting guide

1. Leaves: Paint all leaves green double loaded with
   white, using #2 brush.
2. Roses: Using #2 brush paint half of circle red,
   other half white. Then twirl paint with end of
   brush.
3. Forget-me-nots: Double load with blue and white
   using #2 brush. Paint dots blue. Using same brush
   paint centres yellow and white.
4. Commas: Paint green and white with #00 brush.
5. Edge: Scallops are painted gold using #00 brush.

Follow the same steps for the small bucket.

Finish

Apply 1 coat of gloss finish polyurethane varnish with
12 mm (1") flat brush. Let dry overnight. Apply a
second coat of varnish. Sand gently between coats.

frying pan

bucket

Milk can

Illustrated on page 47

Materials

Small tin milk can
Paints: Waterbased acrylics
Brushes: #4, #2, #00 round brushes; 12 mm and
25 mm (½" and 1") flat brushes
Tracing paper, white transfer paper
Varnish: Polyurethane gloss finish
Pencils: 2B and 5H
Sandpaper: Wet-and-dry #400 or #600

Palette

Base coat: Black
Leaves: Green + white
Tulip: Yellow + white
Roses: Red + white
Cornflower: Mid blue + white
Blue flower: Turquoise + white
Dots: White
Curlicues: Gold
Handles, edges: Highlighted gold

Preparation

1. Apply 1 coat of base coat colour to milk
   can with 12 mm (½") flat brush.
2. Let dry. Sand lightly, apply second coat of base
   coat colour. Let dry.
3. Trace design onto tracing paper.
5. Place pattern onto milk can, slide white transfer
   paper between tracing paper and can.
6. Retrace design with 5H pencil.

Painting guide

1. Leaves: Paint all leaves green and white with #2
   brush.
2. Tulip: Double load #4 brush with yellow and
   white and paint petals.
3. Roses: With #2 brush double load deep red and
   white and paint all petals. Centre of flower is
   painted solid red. White dots are painted with #00
   brush.
4. Cornflower: Double load #2 brush with blue and
   white and paint long strokes on flower.
5. Blue flower: Paint petals with #2 brush double
   loaded blue and white. Centre dots are painted
   yellow.

6. Dots: All dot flowers are painted white with #00
   brush.
7. Curlicues: Paint gold with #00 brush.

Finish

Apply 1 coat of gloss finish polyurethane varnish with
25 mm (1") flat brush. Let dry overnight. Apply a
second coat of varnish. Sand gently between coats.

Paper fan

Illustrated on page 46

Materials

Paper fan
Paints: Waterbased acrylics
Brushes: #6, #2 round brushes; 12 mm and 25 mm
    (½" and 1") flat brushes
Tracing paper, white transfer paper
Varnish: Polyurethane gloss finish
Pencils: 2B and 5H
Sandpaper: Wet-and-dry #400 or #600

Palette

Base coat: Burgundy
Leaves: Green + white
Roses: Pink + white
Dots: Gold

Preparation

1. Apply 1 coat of base coat colour to the fan with 12 mm (½") flat brush.
2. Let dry. Apply second coat of base coat colour. Let dry.
3. Trace design onto tracing paper.
4. Place pattern onto fan, slide white transfer paper between tracing paper and fan.
5. Retrace design with 5H pencil.

Painting guide

1. Leaves: With #2 brush double load green and white and paint all leaves.
2. Roses: Double load #2 brush with pink and white and paint all roses.
3. Dots: Paint solid gold using #2 brush.
4. Dab the #6 brush in gold and spread onto open fan using the dry brush effect

Finish

Apply 1 coat of gloss finish polyurethane varnish with 25 mm (1") flat brush. Let dry overnight. Apply a second coat of varnish. Sand gently between coats.

Small green oval box

Illustrated on page 58

Materials

Small oval balsawood box
Paints: Waterbased acrylics
Brushes: #2, #00, round brushes; 12 mm and
   25 mm (½" and 1") flat brushes
Tracing paper, white transfer paper
Varnish: Polyurethane gloss finish
Pencils: 2B and 5H
Sandpaper: Wet-and-dry #400 or #600

Palette

Base coat: Mid green + dark green
Leaves: Dark green + white
Ducks: White + green + red + black
Hearts: Red
Forget-me-nots: Blue + white + yellow
Bow: Gold
Dots: Gold

Preparation

1. Apply 1 coat of base coat colour to the box with 12 mm (½") flat brush.
2. Let dry. Sand lightly, apply second coat of base coat colour. Let dry.
3. Trace design onto tracing paper.
4. Place pattern onto box, slide white transfer paper between tracing paper and box.
5. Retrace design with 5H pencil.

Painting guide

1. Leaves: Double load green and white; use #00 brush.
2. Ducks: Paint ducks solid white with #2 brush. Add green commas as wings with #2 brush. Paint beak, bows and legs solid red with #00 brush. Eyes paint black with #00 brush.
3. Hearts: Paint solid red with #00 brush.
4. Forget-me-nots: Double load with blue and white using #00 brush. Paint centres yellow and white using same brush.
5. Bow: Paint solid gold with #2 brush.
6. Dots: Using #00 brush paint all dots solid gold.

Finish

Apply 1 coat of gloss finish polyurethane varnish with 25 mm (1") flat brush. Let dry overnight. Apply a second coat of varnish. Sand gently between coats.

Small orange oval box

Illustrated on page 58

Materials

Small oval balsawood box
Paints: Waterbased acrylics
Brushes: #4, #2, #00 round brushes; 12 mm and
    25 mm (½" and 1") flat brushes
Tracing paper, black transfer paper
Varnish: Polyurethane gloss finish
Pencils: 2B and 5H
Sandpaper: Wet-and-dry #400 or #600

Palette

Base coat: Deep orange
Ducks: Bright yellow
Hearts, beaks, cheeks: Red
Eye: Black
Commas: Green + white
Dots: Red + white

Preparation

1. Apply 1 coat of base coat colour to the box with
   12 mm (½") flat brush.
2. Let dry. Sand lightly, apply second coat of base
   coat colour. Let dry.
3. Trace design onto tracing paper.
4. Place pattern onto article, slide the black transfer
   paper between tracing paper and box.
5. Retrace design with 5H pencil.

Painting guide

1. Ducks: With #4 brush paint ducks solid yellow.
2. Hearts, beaks, cheeks: Using #00 brush paint red.
3. Eye: With #00 brush paint eye black.
4. Commas: Double load #2 brush with green and
   white, and paint all commas.
5. Dots: Using #00 brush paint dots red and white.

Finish

Apply 1 coat of gloss finish polyurethane varnish with
25 mm (1") flat brush. Let dry overnight. Apply a
second coat of varnish. Sand gently between coats.

Medium oval box

Illustrated on page 58

Materials

Medium oval balsawood box
Paints: Waterbased acrylics
Brushes: #2, #00 round brushes; 12 mm and 25 mm
   (½" and 1") flat brushes
Tracing paper, white transfer paper
Varnish: Polyurethane gloss finish
Pencils: 2B and 5H
Sandpaper: Wet-and-dry #400 or #600

Palette

Base coat: Black
Leaves: Green + white
Large flowers: White + yellow + red
Daisies: Blue + white + red + yellow
Edge: Gold

Preparation

1. Apply 1 coat of base coat colour to the box with
   12 mm (½") flat brush.
2. Let dry. Sand lightly, apply second coat of base
   coat colour. Let dry.
3. Trace design onto tracing paper.
4. Place pattern onto box, slide white transfer paper
   between tracing paper and box.
5. Retrace design with 5H pencil.

Painting guide

1. Leaves: Paint all leaves with #00 brush loaded
   with green and white.
2. Large flowers: Using #2 brush paint all petals
   solid white. Centre dots yellow and one dot in
   red, use #00 brush.
3. Daisies: Double load blue and white with #2
   brush, paint all petals. Paint larger dots in centre
   yellow, smaller ones red with #2 brush.
4. Edge, scallops: To be painted gold using #2 brush.

Finish

Apply 1 coat of gloss finish polyurethane varnish with
25 mm (1") flat brush. Let dry overnight. Apply a
second coat of varnish. Sand gently between coats.

Opal serviette holder

Illustrated on page 58

Materials

Wooden serviette holder
Paints: Waterbased acrylics
Brushes: #4, #2, #00, round brushes; 12 mm and 25 mm (½" and 1") flat brushes
Tracing paper, black transfer paper
Varnish: Polyurethane satin finish
Pencils: 2B and 5H
Sandpaper: Wet-and-dry #400 or #600

Palette

Base coat: Opal
Leaves: Deep green + white
Commas: Dark green
Violets: Purple + white + yellow + brown
Buds: Purple + white
Dots: White
Curlicues: Gold
Lattice: Gold

Preparation

1. Apply 1 coat of base coat colour to serviette holder with 12 mm (½") flat brush.
2. Let dry. Sand lightly, apply second coat of base coat colour. Let dry.
3. Trace design onto tracing paper.
4. Place pattern onto article, slide the black transfer paper between tracing paper and article.
5. Retrace design with 5H pencil.

Painting guide

1. Leaves: Double load #4 brush with deep green and white and paint all leaves.
2. Commas: With #2 brush paint commas dark green.
3. Violets: Double load #2 brush with purple and white and paint flowers. Using a #00 brush add yellow centre with a touch of brown.
4. Buds: With #2 brush double load purple and white.
5. Dots: Paint white using #00 brush.
6. Curlicues: Paint solid gold using #00 brush.
7. Lattice: Using #00 brush paint gold.

Finish

Apply 1 coat of satin finish polyurethane varnish with 25 mm (1") flat brush. Let dry overnight. Apply a second coat of varnish. Sand gently between coats.

Green serviette holder

Illustrated on page 58

Materials

1 wooden serviette holder
Paints: Waterbased acrylics
Brushes: #4, #2, #00 round brushes; 12 mm and
    25 mm (½" and 1") flat brushes
Tracing paper, white transfer paper
Varnish: Polyurethane satin finish
Pencils: 2B and 5H
Sandpaper: Wet-and-dry #400 or #600

Palette

Base coat: Green oxide
Leaves: Deep green + white
Daisies: Blue + white
Centres: White + yellow + brown
Curlicues: Gold

Preparation

1. Apply 1 coat of base coat colour to serviette holder
    with 12 mm (½") flat brush.
2. Let dry. Sand lightly, apply second coat of base
    coat colour, let dry.
3. Trace design onto tracing paper.
4. Place pattern onto article, slide the white transfer
    paper between tracing paper and article.
5. Retrace design with 5H pencil.

Painting guide

1. Leaves: Double load #2 brush with deep green
    and white and paint all leaves.
2. Daisies: With #4 brush double load with blue
    and white and paint daisies.
3. Centres: Double load white and yellow with #2
    brush and dab gently over circle. Then with #00
    brush add specks of brown here and there to lift
    out centre of flower.
4. Curlicues: Paint gold using #00 brush.

Finish

Apply 1 coat of satin finish polyurethane varnish with
25 mm (1") flat brush. Let dry overnight. Apply a
second coat of varnish. Sand gently between coats.

Oval boxes and serviette holders
(see pages 53–55 and 56–57)

Three little pigs
(see pages 60–62)

Daisy pig

Illustrated on page 59

Materials

Terracotta pig
Paints: Waterbased acrylics
Brushes: #4, #2, #00 round brushes; 12 mm and
   25 mm (½" and 1") flat brushes
Tracing paper, black transfer paper
Varnish: Polyurethane gloss finish
Pencils: 2B and 5H
Sandpaper: Wet-and-dry #400 or #600

Palette

Base coat: Flesh colour
Leaves: Green + white
Stems: Green
Daisies: Blue + white + yellow + brown
Eyes: Black
Cheeks: Soft pink

Preparation

1. Apply 1 coat of base coat colour to the pig with
   12 mm (½") flat brush.
2. Let dry. Sand lightly, apply second coat of base
   coat colour. Let dry.
3. Trace design onto tracing paper.
4. Place pattern onto article, slide the black transfer
   paper between tracing paper and article.
5. Retrace design with 5H pencil.

Painting guide

1. Leaves: Double load #2 brush with green and
   white and paint all leaves.
2. Stems: Paint solid green with #00 brush.
3. Daisies: With #4 brush double load blue and white
   and paint all petals. For centre of flower use #2
   brush and paint yellow and white. With #00 brush
   paint fine dots in centre of flower brown.
4. Eyes: Paint eyes black with #00 brush.
5. Cheeks: With #2 brush paint cheeks soft pink.

Finish

Apply 1 coat of gloss finish polyurethane varnish with
25 mm (1") flat brush. Let dry overnight. Apply a
second coat of varnish.

Rose pig

Illustrated on page 59

Materials

Terracotta pig
Paints: Waterbased acrylics
Brushes: #2, #00 round brushes; 12 mm
and 25 mm (½" and 1") flat brushes
Tracing paper, black transfer paper
Varnish: Polyurethane gloss finish
Pencils: 2B and 5H
Sandpaper: Wet-and-dry #400 or #600

Palette

Base coat: Flesh colour
Large leaves: Medium green + white
Small leaves: Dark green
Roses: Pink + white
Forget-me-nots: Blue + white + yellow
Bow: Pink + white
Eyes: Black
Cheeks: Soft pink

Preparation

1. Apply 1 coat of base coat colour to pig
   with 12 mm (½") flat brush.
2. Let dry. Sand lightly, apply second coat
   of base coat colour. Let dry.
3. Trace design onto tracing paper.
4. Place pattern onto article, slide black
   transfer paper between tracing paper and
   article.
5. Retrace design with 5H pencil.

Painting guide

1. Large leaves: Double load #2 brush with
   medium green and white.
2. Small leaves: With #00 brush paint solid green.
3. Roses: Double load #2 brush with pink and white
   and use comma strokes to paint rose.
4. Forget-me-nots: Using #2 brush double load blue
   and white and paint flowers. With same brush paint
   centres yellow and white.
5. Bow: Double load #2 brush with pink and white.
6. Eyes: Paint eyes black with #00 brush.
7. Cheeks: With #2 brush paint cheeks soft pink.

Finish

Apply 1 coat of gloss finish polyurethane varnish with
25 mm (1") flat brush. Let dry overnight. Apply a
second coat of varnish.

Rosebud pig

Illustrated on page 59

Materials

Terracotta pig
Paints: Waterbased acrylics
Brushes: #2, #00 round brushes; 12 mm and 25 mm
(½" and 1") flat brushes
Tracing paper, black transfer paper
Varnish: Polyurethane gloss finish
Pencils: 2B and 5H
Sandpaper: Wet-and-dry #400 or #600

Palette

Base coat: Flesh colour
Leaves: Green + white
Stems: Green
Rosebuds: Pink + white
Bow: Pink + white
Dots: White
Eyes: Black
Cheeks: Soft pink

Preparation

1. Apply 1 coat of base coat colour to the pig with
   12 mm (½") flat brush.
2. Let dry. Sand lightly, apply second coat of base
   coat colour. Let dry.
3. Trace design onto tracing paper.
4. Place pattern onto article, slide the black transfer
   paper between tracing paper and article.
5. Retrace design with 5H pencil.

Painting guide

1. Leaves: Double load #2 brush with green and
   white.
2. Stems: Paint solid green with #00 brush.
3. Rosebuds: Using #2 brush double load pink and
   white and paint all buds.
4. Bow: Double load pink and white with #2 brush.
5. Dots: Paint white using #00 brush.
6. Eyes: Paint eyes black using #00 brush.
7. Cheeks: With #2 brush paint cheeks soft pink.

Finish

Apply 1 coat of gloss finish polyurethane varnish with
25 mm (1") flat brush. Let dry overnight. Apply a
second coat of varnish.

bow around neck

Large fridge magnets

Illustrated on page 70

Follow the general procedures outlined on previous pages for materials and preparation.

1. *White pig* (diagram p. 64)
Palette

Base coat: White
Hearts: Red
Bow: Gold
Cheeks, mouth: Pink
Eyes: Black

Painting guide

Hearts: With #00 brush paint hearts solid red.
Bow: Paint gold using #4 brush.
Cheeks, mouth: Using #00 brush, paint pink.
Eyes: Solid black using #00 brush.

2. *Boy* (diagram p. 64)
Palette

Base coat: White
Pants: Gold
Hearts: Red
Buttons, lace: Gold

Painting guide

Pants: Paint solid gold using #4 brush.
Hearts: Using #00 brush paint solid red.
Buttons, lace: With #00 brush paint solid gold.

3. *Girl* (diagram p. 64)
Palette

Base coat: White
Hearts: Red
Bow: Gold
Lace, ribbon: Gold

Painting guide

Hearts: Paint solid red using #00 brush.
Bow: Using #2 brush paint gold.
Lace, ribbon: Paint gold using #00 brush.

4. *Cat* (diagram p. 64)
Palette

Base coat: Black
Bow: Red
Dots: White

Painting guide

Bow: Using #00 brush paint bow solid red.
Dots: Paint white using #00 brush.

5. *Duck with heart* (diagram p. 64)
Palette

Base coat heart: Red
Base coat duck: White
Bow, beak: Red
Dots: Red
Commas: Green
Half circle: Blue

Painting guide

Bow, beak: Using #2 brush paint solid red.
Dots: With #00 brush paint red.
Commas: Paint solid green using #00 brush.
Half circle: Using #2 brush paint solid blue.

6. *Strawberry* (diagram p. 64)
Palette

Base coat: Red
Leaves: Green + gold
Seeds: Gold + brown

Painting guide

Leaves: Paint solid green using #4 brush. Outline with gold using #00 brush.
Seeds: Using #00 brush paint commas solid gold. Then outline one side with brown using same brush.

7. *Apple* (diagram p. 64)
Palette

Base coat: Red
Leaves: Green
Hole: Gold + black
Grub: Green + black

Painting guide

Leaves: Paint solid green using #2 brush.
Hole: Using #2 brush paint the hole solid gold. Outline hole in black using #00 brush.
Grub: Paint solid green using #2 brush. Highlight with black and gold using #00 brush.

8. *Swan* (diagram p. 64)

Palette

Base coat: White
Commas: Green + white
Beak, cheeks: Red
Eyes: Black

Painting guide

Commas: Double load green and white using #2 brush.
Beak, cheeks: Paint beak solid red using #2 brush. For cheeks use dry brush effect using #00 brush.
Eyes: Paint solid black using #00 brush.

9. *Basket* (diagram p. 64)

Palette

Base coat: Dark green
Leaves: Light green + white
Flowers: Blue + yellow + white
Bow: Blue + white
Dots: White

Painting guide

Leaves: Double load green and white using #00 brush.
Flowers: Double load #2 brush in blue and white. For centres use #00 brush and paint yellow with a touch of white.
Bow: Double load blue and white using #2 brush.
Dots: Paint white using #00 brush.

10. *Duck with blue coat* (diagram p. 65)

Palette

Base coat: White
Blue parts: Blue + white
Commas: Green + white
Beak, feet: Red
Cheeks: Red
Eyes: Black

Painting guide

Blue parts: Paint solid blue using #4 brush. Add white dots to bow using #00 brush. Add fine lines in white to half circle using #00 brush.
Commas: Double load green and white using #2 brush.
Beak, feet: Paint solid red using #2 brush.
Cheeks: With dry brush effect paint red using #00 brush.
Eyes: Paint black using #00 brush.

11. *Duck with red coat* (diagram p. 65)

Palette

Base coat: White
Red parts: Red + white
Commas: Green + white
Beak, feet: Red
Cheeks: Red
Eyes: Black

Painting guide

Red parts: Paint solid red using #4 brush. Add white dots to bow using #00 brush. Add fine lines in white to half circle using #00 brush.
Commas: Double load green and white using #2 brush.
Beak, feet: Paint solid red using #2 brush.
Cheeks: Using dry brush effect paint red using #00 brush.
Eyes: Paint black using #00 brush.

12. *Soldier* (diagram p. 65)

Palette

Base coat: Red
Hat: Black
Jacket: Red + black
Pants: Blue
Shoes: Black
Buttons, hands: White
Cheeks, mouth: Red

Painting guide

Hat: Paint solid black using #4 brush.
Jacket: Paint solid red using #4 brush. Add black outlines using #00 brush.
Pants: Using #2 brush paint solid blue. Add black line down centre with #00 brush.
Shoes: Paint solid black using #2 brush.
Buttons, hands: Using #00 brush paint white.
Cheeks, mouth: Paint red using #00 brush.

13. Sheep (diagram p. 65)

Palette

Base coat: White
Leaves: Gold
Roses: Gold
Hearts: Gold
Dots: Gold

Painting guide

Leaves: Using #00 brush paint all leaves solid gold.
Roses: With #2 brush paint gold using comma strokes.
Hearts: Paint gold using #00 brush.
Dots: Gold using #00 brush.

14. Rocking horse (diagram p. 65)

Palette

Base coat: Blue
Saddle, bottom: Red
Commas: Grey + white
Dots: White
Eyes: Black

Painting guide

Saddle, bottom: Paint solid red using #4 brush. Add white lines and dots with #00 brush.
Commas: Double load grey and white using #2 brush.
Dots: Paint white using #00 brush.
Eyes: Solid black using #00 brush.

15. House (diagram p. 65)

Palette

Base coat: Brown
Roof: Red
Windows: Red + Green
Leaves: Green + white
Flowers: White

Painting guide

Roof: Paint solid red using #4 brush.
Windows: Using #2 brush paint solid red, then add fine green lines as highlights with #00 brush.
Leaves: Double load green and white using #00 brush.
Flowers: Paint white using #00 brush.

16. Pink pig (diagram p. 65)

Palette

Base coat: Pink
Flowers: Light pink + white
Nose, ears, tail: Pink + white
Eyes: Brown

Painting guide

Flowers: Double load pink and white with #00 brush. For centres; use same brush and paint white.
Nose, ears, tail: Double load #2 brush with pink and white.
Eyes: Paint solid brown using #00 brush. Add white highlight.

17. Black cat (diagram p. 68)

Palette

Base coat: Black
Commas: Blue + white
Scarf: Red + white
Mouth, cheeks: Red
Whiskers, eyes: Grey

Painting guide

Commas: Using #2 brush double load blue and white.
Scarf: Paint scarf red using #2 brush. Paint white dots with #00 brush.
Mouth, cheeks: Using #00 brush paint red.
Whiskers, eyes: Paint grey using # 00 brush.

18. Cow (diagram p. 68)

Palette

Base coat: White + brown
Flowers: Blue + white
Leaves: Green + white
Eyes, nose: Black + white

Painting guide

Flowers: Double load blue and white using #00 brush.
Leaves: With #00 brush double load green and white.
Eyes, nose: Paint solid black with #00 brush. Add white for highlights.

19. Grey mouse (diagram p. 68)

Palette

Base coat: Grey
Commas: Green + white
Bow tie, ears: Blue + white
Eyes, nose: Black + white
Whiskers: Black
Cheeks: Red

17

18

19

20

21

22

23

Painting guide

Commas: Double load green and white using #2 brush.
Bow tie, ears: Paint solid blue with #2 brush. Paint white dots with #00 brush. For ears, double load blue and white with #2 brush.
Eyes, nose: Paint black with #00 brush. Add white for highlights with same brush.
Whiskers: Black using #00 brush.
Cheeks: Paint red using #00 brush using dry brush effect.

20. Teddy bear (diagram p. 68)

Palette

Base coat: Dark brown
Pads on bear: Light brown + white
Bow: Light blue + white
Eyes, nose: Black + white
Cheeks: Soft pink

Painting guide

Bears' pads: With #2 brush double load light brown and white.
Bow: Double load light blue and white with #00 brush and paint bow.
Eyes, nose: Solid black using #00 brush. Add details to eyes using a touch of white with #00 brush.
Cheeks: With #00 brush paint soft pink with dry brush effect.

21. Standing duck (diagram p. 68)

Palette

Base coat: White
Beak, feet, buttons: Red
Commas: Green + yellow
Eyes: Black + white
Cheeks: Red

Painting guide

Beak, feet, buttons: Paint solid red using #2 brush.
Commas: First paint yellow with #2 brush, when dry go over half of yellow with green using same brush.
Eyes: Paint solid black with #00 brush. Add a touch of white.
Cheeks: Paint red with #00 brush using dry brush effect.

22. Cream duck (diagram p. 68)

Palette

Base coat: Cream
Rose: Orange + white
Leaves: Green + white
Commas: Green + white
Beak: Orange
Cheeks: Soft pink
Eyes: Black + white

Painting guide

Rose: Double load orange and white using #2 brush.
Leaves: Using #00 brush double load green and white and paint all leaves.
Commas: With #2 brush double load green and white paint all commas.
Beak: Paint solid orange using #2 brush.
Cheeks: With #00 brush paint soft pink using dry brush effect.
Eyes: Paint black with #00 brush. Add life to eyes with a touch of white.

23. White goose, head down

(diagram p. 68)

Palette

Base coat: White
Commas: Green + white
Beak, feet: Red
Wing, scarf: Yellow
Hearts, dots: Red
Eyes: Black
Cheeks: Red

Painting guide

Commas: Double load green and white with #2 brush.
Beak, feet: Paint solid red using #2 brush.
Wing, scarf: Solid yellow using #4 brush.
Hearts, dots: Paint heart red using #2 brush. Dots red using #00 brush.
Eyes: Using #00 brush paint black.
Cheeks: Paint red using #00 brush.

Finish

Glue magnets to backs of shapes with strong craft glue or Supa-Glue.

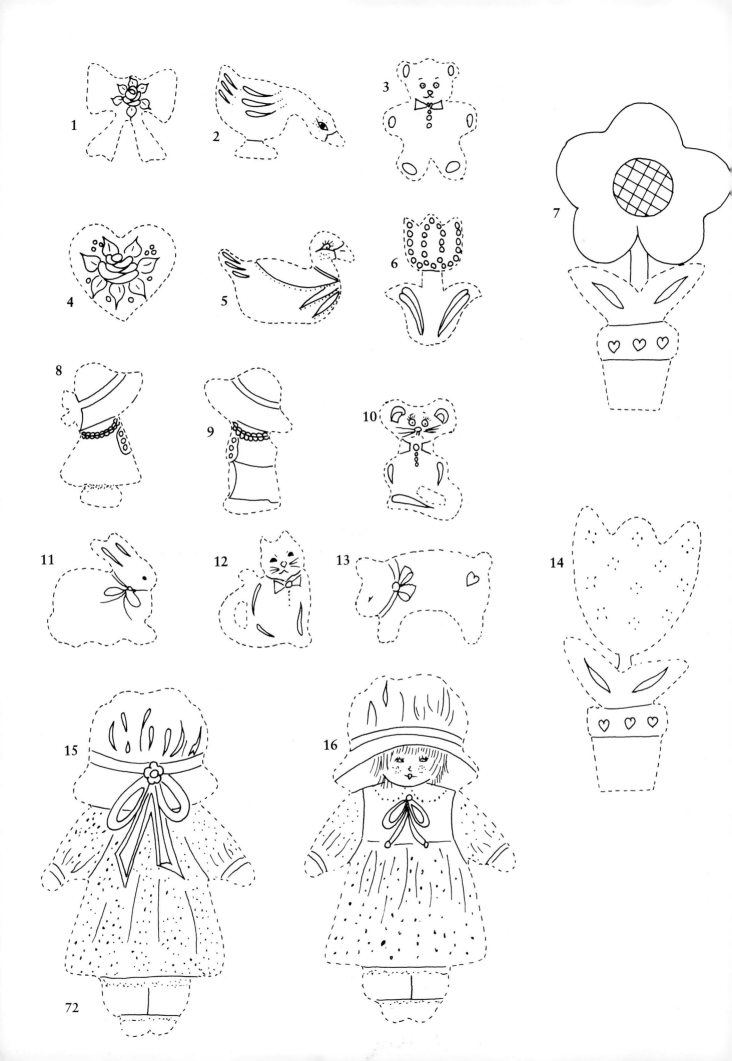

1

2

3

7

4

5

6

8

9

10

11

12

13

14

15

16

72

Small fridge magnets

Illustrated on page 71

Follow the general procedures outlined on previous pages for materials and preparation.

1. Red bow

Palette

Base coat: Bright red
Rose: Red + white
Leaves: Green + white

Painting guide

Rose: Double load red and white with #2 brush.
Leaves: Using #00 brush paint leaves green and white.

2. Plum pink goose

Palette

Base coat: Plum pink
Wings, feet: Gold
Eye: Black + white

Painting guide

Wings, feet, beak: Paint gold using #2 brush.
Eye: Paint black using #00 brush. Add white for highlight.

3. Small teddy bear

Palette

Bow tie: Pink
Pads: Gold + white
Buttons: Gold
Eyes, nose: Black + brown + white

Painting guide

Bow tie: Paint pink and white using #00 brush.
Pads: Double load gold and white with #00 brush.
Buttons: Paint solid gold using #00 brush.
Eyes, nose: Paint black, add a touch of white, then outline with brown using #00 brush.

4. Pink heart

Palette

Base coat: Pale pink
Rose: Pink + white
Leaves: Green
Dots: Gold

Painting guide

Rose: Double load pink and white using #2 brush.
Leaves: Paint green with #00 brush.
Dots: Paint gold using #00 brush.

5. Yellow duck

Palette

Base coat: Bright yellow
Scarf, beak: Red
Eyes: Black
Commas, dots: Green

Painting guide

Scarf, beak, cheeks: Paint red using #2 brush.
Eyes: Black using #00 brush.
Commas: Using #00 brush paint green.

6. Small tulip

Palette

Tulip: Red
Leaves: Green + light green + gold
Dots: White

Painting guide

Tulip: Paint tulip red using #2 brush.
Leaves: Paint medium green first. Let dry then add two comma strokes in gold and light green using #00 brush.
Dots: Paint white using same brush.

7. Daisy in pot

Palette

Flower: Blue
Pot: Terracotta
Leaves: Green
Hearts: Red
Centre: Yellow + red + brown

Painting guide

Flower: Paint solid blue using #4 brush.
Pot: With #2 brush paint terracotta.
Leaves: Using #2 brush paint leaves green.
Hearts: Solid red using #00 brush.
Centre: Paint solid yellow. When dry add fine brown lines in centre using #00 brush. Add red dots last.

8 & 9. Tiny girl and boy

Palette

Hats, pants: Blue
Dress, shirt: White
Buttons, lace: Gold

Painting guide

Hats, pants: With #2 brush paint blue.
Dress, shirt: Paint white with #2 brush.
Buttons, lace: Using #00 brush paint gold.

10. Black mouse

Palette

Base coat: Black
Bow tie: White
Ears: Pink
Eyes: Blue

Painting guide

Bow tie: Paint white using #00 brush.
Ears: Using same brush paint pink.
Eyes: Solid blue, with a touch of black and white.

11. White rabbit

Palette

Heart, bow: Red
Commas: Red
Eye: Black

Painting guide

Heart, bow: Paint red using #00 brush.
Commas: Using same brush paint red.
Eye: Solid black with #00 brush.

12. Grey cat

Palette

Base coat: Grey
Commas, bow tie: Blue + white
Eyes, nose: Black
Whiskers: Black

Painting guide

Commas, bow tie: Double load blue and white with #00 brush.
Eyes: Paint black, then add white.
Whiskers: With #00 brush paint black.

13. Black pig

Palette

Heart, bow: Red
Eye: Black

Painting guide

Heart, bow: Paint red using #00 brush.
Eye: White using #00 brush

14. Tulip in pot

Palette

Base coat: Red
Leaves: Green
Pot: Terracotta
Hearts: Red
Dots: White

Painting guide

Tulip: Paint solid red using #4 brush.
Leaves: Using #2 brush paint green.
Pot: With #2 brush paint terracotta.
Hearts: Paint solid red using #00 brush.
Dots: White using #00 brush.

15 & 16. Pink girls

Palette

Dress, shoes: Light pink
Hat, lace, bow: White
Hair: Brown
Eyes: Brown + white

Painting guide

Dress, shoes: Paint light pink using #4 brush. Add white dots to dress with #00 brush. Reverse these colours for the back view.
Hat, lace, bow: Paint solid white using #2 brush. Add pink band to hat with same brush.
Hair: Paint brown with #00 brush.
Eyes: Brown with #00 brush.

Finish

Glue magnets to backs of shapes with strong craft glue or Supa-Glue.

Black cats and hearts

Cats illustrated on page 82

Materials

Wooden cats
Paints: Waterbased acrylics
Brushes: #2, #00 round brushes; 12 mm and 25 mm
   (½" and 1") flat brushes
Varnish: Polyurethane gloss finish
Pencils: 2B and 5H
Sandpaper: Wet-and-dry #400 or #600

Palette

Base coat: Black
Bow: Blue
Rose: Pink + white
Leaves: Green + white

Preparation

1. Apply 1 coat of base coat colour to the cats with
   12 mm (½") flat brush.
2. Let dry. Sand lightly, apply second coat of base
   coat colour. Let dry.

Painting guide

1. Bow: Paint tiny bows solid blue with #2 brush.
2. Rose: Double load pink and white with #2 brush
   and paint roses.
3. Leaves: Using #00 brush paint leaves, double loading green and white.

Finish for cats and hearts

Apply 1 coat of gloss finish polyurethane varnish with
25 mm (1") flat brush. Let dry, preferably overnight.
Apply a second coat of varnish. Sand gently between
coats. Glue string to hearts.

Decorating suggestions

1. Stand black cats on a long shelf; stand a heart at
   each end.
2. Place cats along top of doorway.
3. Stand cats in a group on corner shelf.
4. Attach hearts on string to cat's paw and place the
   cat at the end of the shelf.

Hearts illustrated on page 82

Materials

Wooden hearts
Paints: Waterbased acrylics
Brushes: #2 round brush; 12 mm and 25 mm (½"
   and 1") flat brushes
Varnish: Polyurethane gloss finish
Pencils: 2B and 5H
Sandpaper: Wet-and-dry #400 or #600

Palette

Base coat: Black
Inner heart: Red

Preparation

1. Apply 1 coat of base coat colour to the hearts with
   12 mm (½") flat brush.
2. Let dry. Sand lightly, apply second coat of base
   coat colour. Let dry.
3. Trace design onto tracing paper.
4. Place pattern onto article, slide the black transfer
   paper between tracing paper and article.
5. Retrace design with 5H pencil.

Painting guide

1. Outer hearts: Paint these solid black on both sides;
   use #2 brush.
2. Inner hearts: Paint solid red with #2 brush.

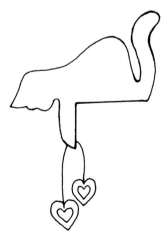

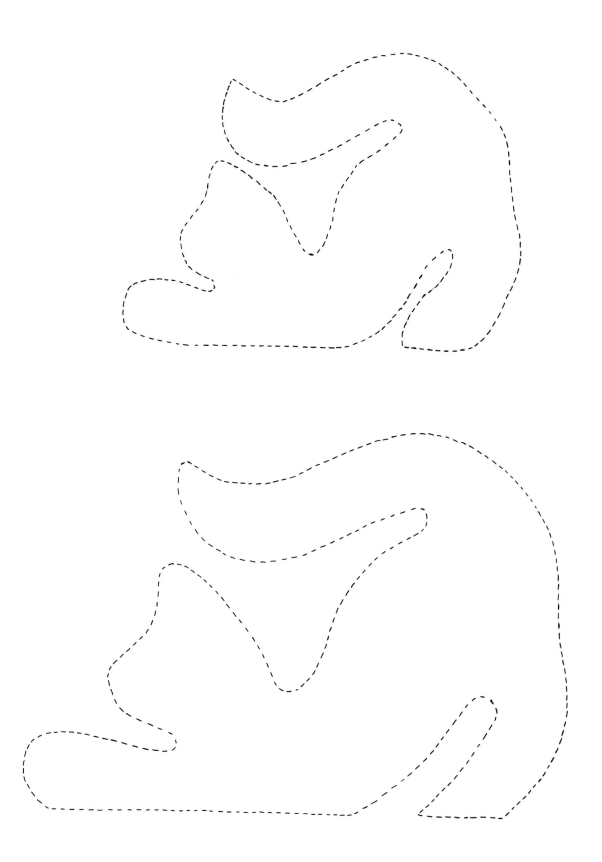

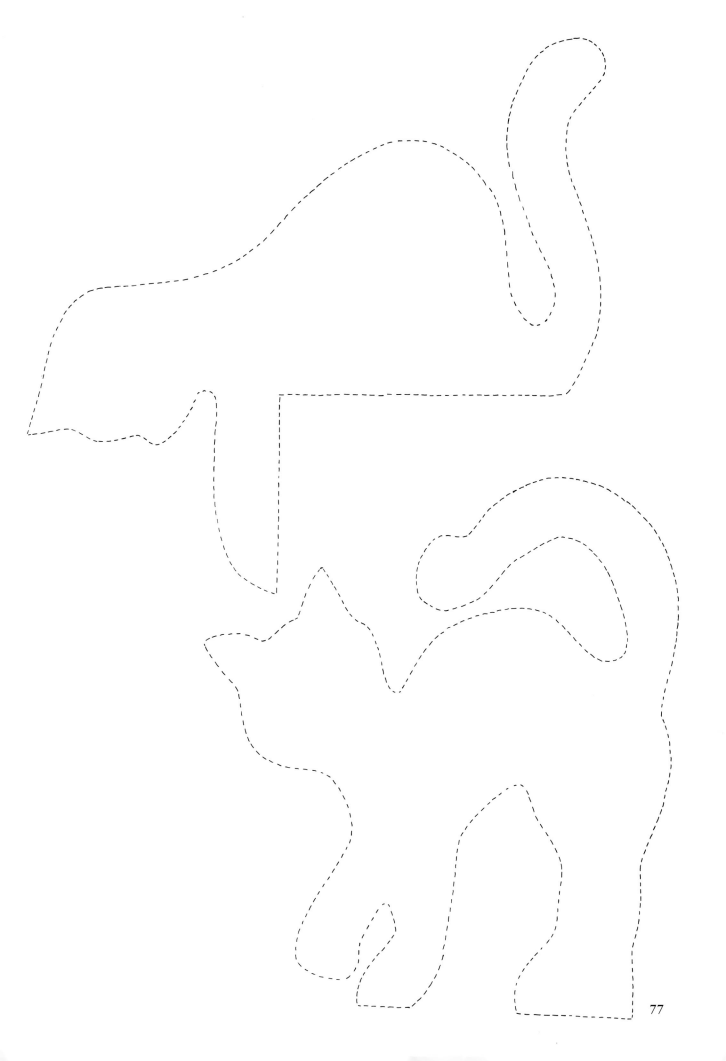

77

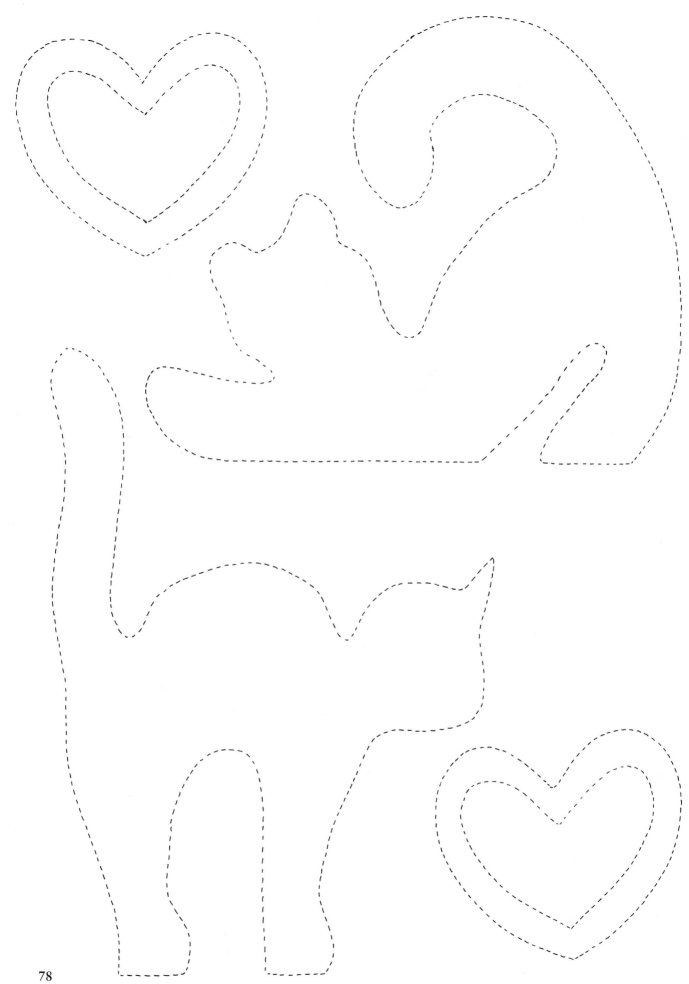

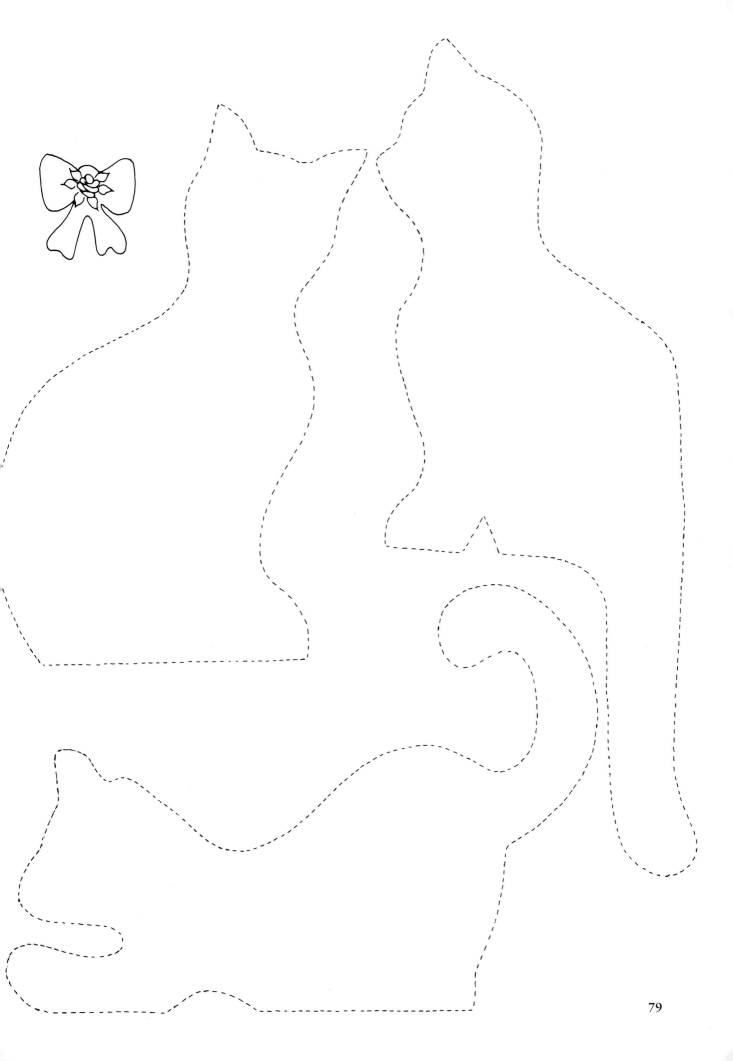

Poppies kitchen set

Illustrated on page 83

Materials

Wooden tray, bread board, mortar & pestle, salt grinder, mustard pot, vase, butter dish, and candle holders

Paints: Waterbased acrylics

Brushes: #4, #2, #00 round brushes; 12 mm and 25 mm (½" and 1") flat brushes

Tracing paper, black transfer paper

Varnish: Polyurethane gloss finish

Pencils: 2B and 5H

Sandpaper: Wet-and-dry #400 or #600

Palette

Base coat: White
Leaves: Dark green
Poppies: Bright red
Centre: Dark red + green
Details: Black

Preparation

1. Apply 1 coat of base coat colour to kitchen set with 12 mm (½") flat brush.
2. Let dry. Sand lightly. Apply second coat of base coat colour. Let dry.
3. Trace design onto tracing paper. Reduce the smaller design as required to fit the candle holders.
4. Place the patterns onto articles, slide the black transfer paper between tracing paper and articles.
5. Retrace design with 5H pencil.

Painting guide

1. Leaves: Paint all leaves dark green using #4 brush.
2. Using #4 brush first paint poppies bright red, then add dark red to inner part of flower using same brush.
3. Paint centres dark red and green using #2 brush.
4. Details: All fine details are to be painted in black using #00 brush.

Finish

Apply 1 coat of gloss finish polyurethane varnish with 25 mm (1") flat brush. Let dry, preferably overnight. Apply second coat of varnish. If you wish you may add a third coat of varnish.

Black cats
(see pages 75–79)

Poppies kitchen set
(see page 80)

Wooden poppy box and spoon

Illustrated on page 90

Materials

Wooden box and spoon
Paints: Waterbased acrylics
Brushes: #4, #2, #00 round brushes; 12 mm and
   25 mm (½" and 1") flat brushes
Tracing paper, black transfer paper
Varnish: Polyurethane gloss finish
Pencils: 2B and 5H
Sandpaper: Wet-and-dry #400 or #600

Palette

Leaves: Light green + dark green + black
Poppies: Bright red + dark red + black + green

Preparation

1. Apply wood stain to box and spoon.
2. Let dry. Sand lightly.
3. Trace design onto tracing paper.
4. Place pattern onto articles, slide black transfer paper between tracing paper and articles.
5. Retrace design with 5H pencil.

Painting guide

1. Leaves: First paint leaves light green with #2 brush. Then add details with dark green using same brush. Lastly add black lines to leaves using #00 brush.
2. Poppies: With #4 brush paint poppies solid bright red. Then add dark red parts to flower using same brush. Centre is to be painted light and dark green with #2 brush. All details paint black using #00 brush.

Finish

Apply 1 coat of gloss finish polyurethane varnish with 25 mm (1") flat brush. Let dry, preferably overnight. Apply a second coat of varnish.

Duck tea towels

Illustrated on page 90

Important: When painting on fabric add textile medium to all paints. This stops the paint bleeding into the surrounding fabric.

Bright yellow ducks
Palette

Beaks, feet: Bright red
Wings: Blue
Dots: White
Eyes: Black with a touch of white
Cheeks: Red
Heart: Blue
Flowers: Blue
Leaves: Green

Painting guide

Ducks: Paint ducks bright yellow using #4 brush.
Beaks and feet: Using #2 brush paint solid bright red.
Wings: With #4 brush paint wings blue.
Dots: Dots on wings are painted solid white using #00 brush.
Eyes: Using #00 brush paint eyes black using #00 brush. Paint a white dot in the centre of eye.
Cheeks: Paint red with a dry brush effect using #00 brush.
Heart: Solid blue using #2 brush.
Flowers: Using #00 brush paint all flowers blue.
Leaves: Paint green using #00 brush.

Grey ducks (diagram p. 88)
Palette

Bow, beak: Burgundy
Cheeks: Burgundy
Eyes: Black
Wings: Burgundy
Dots: White
Feet: Burgundy
Heart: Burgundy
Flowers: Burgundy
Leaves: Green

Painting guide

1. Bow, beak: Using #2 brush paint burgundy.
2. Cheeks: With #00 brush paint cheeks burgundy using a dry brush effect.
3. Eyes: Paint eyes black, then add white dot in centre using #00 brush.
4. Wings: Using #4 brush paint burgundy. For white dots in wing use #00 brush.
5. Feet and heart: Paint burgundy using #2 brush.
6. Flowers: Using #2 brush paint all flowers burgundy.
7. Leaves: Paint solid green using #2 brush.

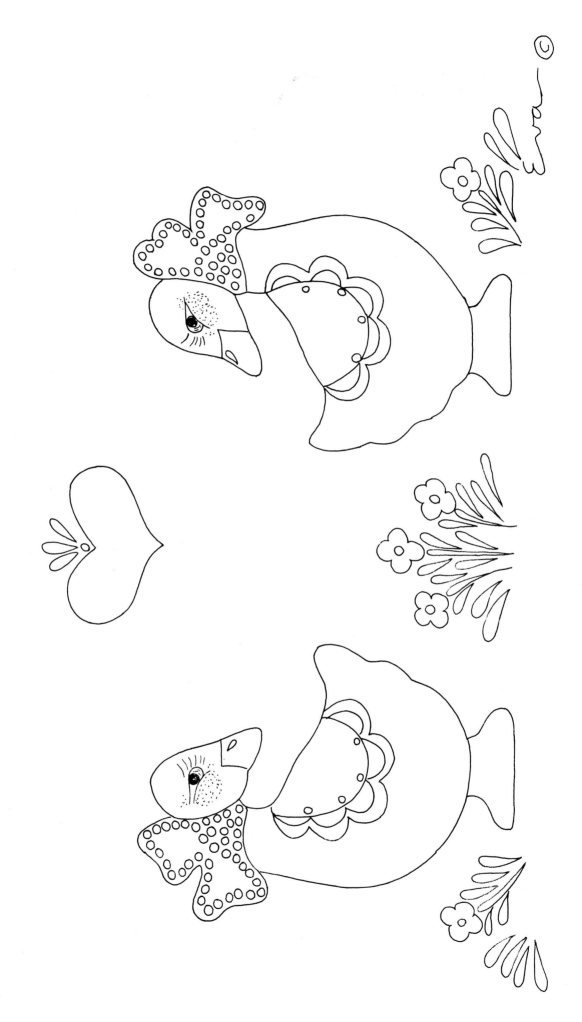

Miniature milk can

Illustrated on page 91

Materials

Metal milk can
Paints: Waterbased acrylics
Brushes: #2, #1, #00 round brushes; 12 mm and
    25 mm (½" and 1") flat brushes
Tracing paper, white transfer paper
Varnish: Polyurethane gloss finish
Pencils: 2B and 5H
Sandpaper: Wet-and-dry #400 or #600

Palette

Base coat: Deep green + burgundy
Leaves: Light green + white
Flowers: White + yellow + green
Strawberries: Deep red + yellow + white + brown

Preparation

1. Apply 1 coat of deep green base coat to milk can
   with 12 mm (½") flat brush. Base coat handles in
   burgundy.
2. Let dry. Sand lightly, apply second coats of base
   coat colours. Let dry.
3. Trace design onto tracing paper.
4. Place pattern onto milk can, slide white transfer
   paper between tracing paper and can.
5. Retrace design with 5H pencil.

Painting guide

1. Leaves: Using #1 brush double load light green
   and white and paint all leaves.
2. Flowers: With #2 brush first paint flowers light
   green. When dry paint over with white using same
   brush. Paint centres yellow and white using #1
   brush.
3. Strawberries: First paint solid deep red using #2
   brush. With same brush load deep red; yellow and
   white and paint over undercoat. Paint seeds white
   with a dash of brown with #00 brush.

Finish

Apply 1 coat of gloss finish polyurethane varnish with
25 mm (1") flat brush. Let dry overnight. Apply a
second coat of varnish. Sand gently between coats.

top front

lid

front

Wooden poppy box, tea towels and spoon
(see pages 85 and 86)

*Miniature milk can, bucket and tub
(see pages 89, 92–93)*

Small oval tub

Illustrated on page 91

Materials

Metal tub
Paints: Waterbased acrylics
Brushes: #4, #2, #00 round brushes; 12 mm and
   25 mm (½" and 1") flat brushes
Tracing paper, white transfer paper
Varnish: Polyurethane gloss finish
Pencils: 2B and 5H
Sandpaper: Wet-and-dry #400 or #600

Palette

Base coat: Black
Leaves: Mid green + white
Daisies: Blue + white
Centres: Yellow + white + brown
Dots: Gold
Highlights: Gold

Preparation

1. Apply 1 coat of base coat colour to bucket with
   12 mm (½") flat brush.
2. Let dry. Sand lightly; apply second coat of base
   coat colour. Let dry.
3. Trace design onto tracing paper.
4. Place pattern onto article, slide the white transfer
   paper between tracing paper and article.
5. Retrace design with 5H pencil.

Painting guide

1. Leaves: Double load green and white with #4
   brush and paint all leaves.
2. Daisies: With #2 brush double load blue and
   white, paint all flowers.
3. Centres: Paint centres yellow with a touch of white
   here and there. Using #00 brush add fine brown
   dots to 'lift' the centre.
4. Dots: Paint solid gold using #00 brush.
5. Highlights: Paint solid gold using #4 brush. You
   will need two coats.

Finish

Apply 1 coat of gloss finish polyurethane varnish with
25 mm (1") flat brush to article. Let dry, preferably
overnight. Apply a second coat of varnish.

Metal bucket

Illustrated on page 91

Materials

Medium metal bucket
Paints: Waterbased acrylics
Brushes: #4, #2, #00 round brushes; 12 mm and 25 mm (½" and 1") flat brushes
Tracing paper, white transfer paper
Varnish: Polyurethane gloss finish
Pencils: 2B and 5H
Sandpaper: Wet-and-dry #400 or #600

Palette

Base coat: Black
Leaves: Green + white
Stems: Green
Flowers: Blue + white
Heart: Red
Lines: Gold
Birds: Turquoise + mid blue
Eyes: Black

Preparation

1. Apply 1 coat of base coat colour to bucket with 12 mm (½") flat brush.
2. Let dry. Sand lightly, apply second coat of base coat colour. Let dry.
3. Trace design onto tracing paper.
4. Place pattern onto bucket, slide the white transfer paper between tracing paper and article.
5. Retrace design with 5H pencil.

Painting guide

1. Leaves: Double load green and white and paint all leaves with #00 brush.
2. Stems: Using #00 brush paint all stems green.
3. Flowers: With #2 brush double load blue and white and paint all flowers.
4. Heart: Paint solid red using #4 brush.
5. Lines: Lines in heart paint gold using #00 brush.
6. Birds: Paint birds solid turquoise and mid blue using #4 brush. Paint dots on tails gold with #00 brush.
7. Eyes: Using #00 brush paint eyes black.

Finish

Apply 1 coat of gloss finish polyurethane varnish with 25 mm (1") flat brush. Let dry, preferably overnight. Apply a second coat of varnish.

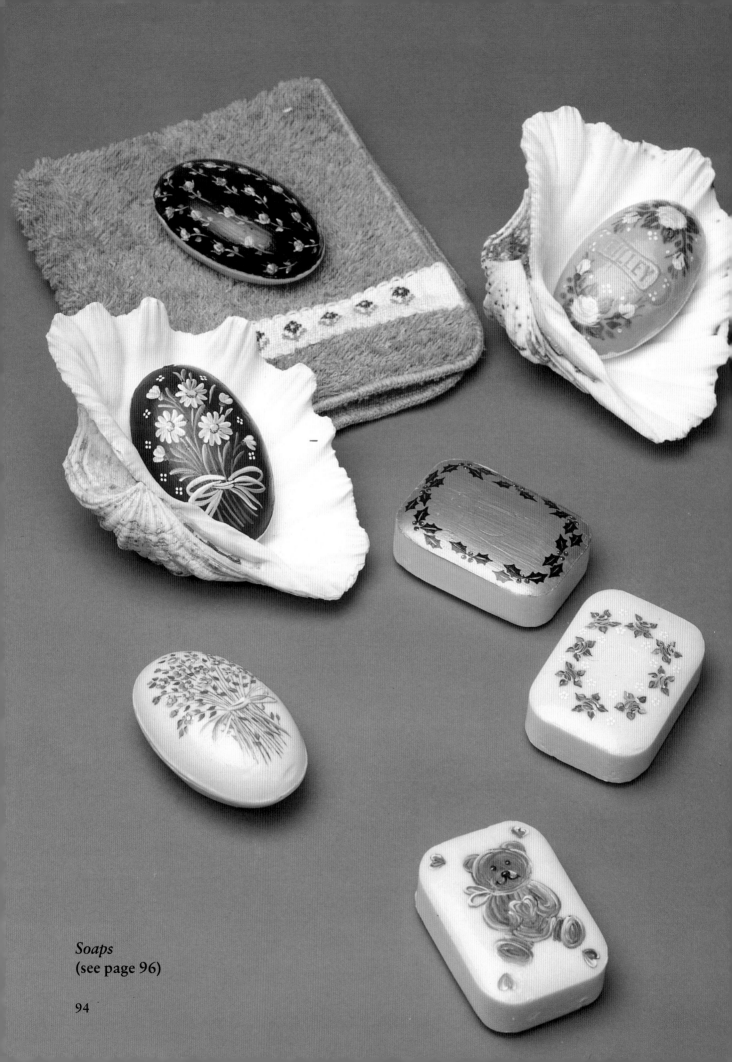

Soaps
(see page 96)

94

*Terracotta pots
and wooden spoons
(see pages 98
and 100)*

Soaps

Illustrated on page 94

Preparation
Apply 1 coat of all purpose sealer to soaps and allow to let dry before painting.

Soap 1
Palette
Base coat: Deep blue 2 coats
Leaves: Green + white
Daisies: Pale blue + white + yellow + brown
Bow: Pale blue + white
Dots: White

Painting guide
Leaves: With #2 brush paint all leaves, double loading green and white.
Daisies: Double load pale blue and white and paint all flowers with #2 brush. Add white and yellow centres using same brush. Add brown dots to highlight centre of flower, using #00 brush.
Dots: With #00 brush paint white.

Soap 2
Palette
Base coat: Dark green
Rosebuds: Pink + white
Stems, leaves: Green + white

Painting guide
Rosebuds: Double load pink and white with #00 brush and paint all flowers.
Stems, leaves: With same brush double load green and white and paint all leaves.

Soap 3
Palette
Base coat: Gold
Holly leaves: Dark green
Berries: Red + white

Painting guide
Holly leaves: Paint solid dark green using #00 brush.
Berries: Double load red and white and paint all berries with #00 brush.

Soap 4
Palette
Teddy bear: Brown + white
Bow, hearts: Blue + white
Eyes, nose: Black

Painting guide
Teddy bear: Double load brown and white; use #2 brush.
Bow, hearts: With #2 brush double load blue and white.
Eyes, nose: Paint black with #00 brush.

Soap 5
Palette
Leaves: Green + white
Roses: Pink + white
Dots: White

Painting guide
Leaves: With #2 brush double load green and white.
Roses: Double load pink and white; use #2 brush.
Dots: White with #00 brush.

Soap 6
Palette
Base coat: Soft pink
Leaves: Green + brown
Rosebuds: Soft pink + white
Dots: White

Painting guide
Leaves: Double load green and brown with #2 brush.
Rosebuds: Double load soft pink and white; use #00 brush.
Dots: With #00 brush paint white.

Soap 7
Palette
Stems, leaves: Green
Forget-me-nots: Blue + white + yellow + brown
Bow: Blue + white

Painting guide
Stems, leaves: With #2 brush paint green.
Forget-me-nots: Double load blue and white; use #2 brush.
Centre paint yellow with a touch of brown; use #2 brush.
Bow: Double load blue and white with #2 brush.

Terracotta pots

Illustrated on page 95

Pot 1

Palette

Base coat: Antique pink
Leaves: Green + white
Roses: Pink + white
Forget-me-nots: Blue + white + yellow
Dots: White

Painting guide

1. Leaves: Double load green and white and paint all leaves.
2. Roses: Using #2 brush double load pink and white.
3. Forget-me-nots: Double load blue and white paint all flowers with #00 brush. Centres paint yellow and white using #00 brush.
4. Dots: Paint solid white using #00 brush.

Pot 2

Palette

Base coat: Antique blue
Strawberries: Red + white
Leaves: Green + white
Flowers: White + green + yellow
Curls: Gold

Painting guide

1. Strawberries: Double load #2 brush with red and white and paint all strawberries. Seeds are yellow and brown, painted with #00 brush.
2. Leaves: Double load #2 brush with green and white.
3. Flowers: Paint solid white first. Then double load pale green and white with #2 brush. Yellow dots in centre are painted with #00 brush.

Pot 3

Palette

Base coat: Burgundy
Ducks: Grey + white + burgundy
Leaves: Green + white
Roses: Burgundy + white
Dots: White

Painting guide

1. Ducks: Paint solid grey with #4 brush. Add white commas for wings with #00 brush. Add large white half circle for back with #4 brush. Burgundy criss-cross is done with #00 brush.
2. Feet: Solid gold with #2 brush.
3. Leaves: Double load green and white with #2 brush.
4. Roses: With #2 brush double load burgundy and white.
5. Dots: Paint white with #00 brush.

1

2

3

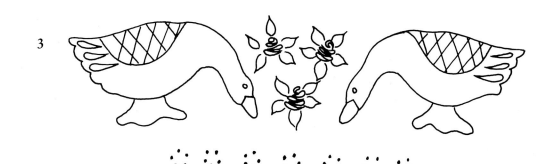

Wooden spoons

Illustrated on page 95

Materials

Four wooden spoons
Paints: Waterbased acrylics
Brushes: #4, #2, #00 round brushes; 12 mm and
  25 mm (½" and 1") flat brushes
Tracing paper, white transfer paper
Varnish: Polyurethane gloss finish
Pencils: 2B and 5H
Sandpaper: Wet-and-dry #400 or #600

Follow the general procedures outlined on previous
pages for materials and preparation.

1. Turquoise spoon
Palette

Base coat: Turquoise
Leaves: Green
Rose: Dark pink + light pink + white
Forget-me-nots: Blue + yellow

Painting guide

Leaves: With #4 brush paint all leaves solid green.
Rose: Paint bowl part of rose solid dark pink with #4
brush. When dry double load light pink and white and
paint rose again with #2 brush.
Forget-me-nots: Using #00 brush paint flowers solid
blue and centres solid yellow.

2. Green spoon
Palette

Base coat: Green
Leaves: Light green + dark green
Tulips: Bright red + blue
Dots: Yellow

Painting guide

Leaves: Paint light green with #2 brush. When dry
add dark green comma inside leaf with #00 brush.
Tulips: Using #2 brush paint all tulips solid red. Add
blue comma on top of tulip with #00 brush.
Dots: Solid yellow using #00 brush.

3. Antique blue spoon
Palette

Base coat: Antique blue
Leaves: Light green
Roses: Dark pink + light pink + white
Comma strokes: Light pink + white

Painting guide

Leaves: Paint solid green with #4 brush.
Roses: First paint dark pink base with #4 brush.
Commas: Double load light pink and white with #2
brush and paint all petals.

4. Dark blue spoon
Palette

Base coat: Dark blue
Leaves: Green
Daisies: White + yellow
Hearts: Red
Leaves: Paint solid green with #00 brush.
Daisies: Solid white using #2 brush. Paint centres
yellow with #00 brush.
Hearts: Paint solid red using #2 brush.

Finish

Apply 1 coat of gloss finish polyurethane varnish with
25 mm (1") flat brush. Let dry overnight. Apply a
second coat of varnish. Sand between coats.

101

Large Christmas decorations

Illustrated on page 106

Follow the general procedures outlined on previous pages for materials and preparation.

1. Snowflake
Palette

Base coat: Silver
Leaves: Dark green
Berries: Red

Painting guide

Leaves: Paint leaves dark green using #00 brush.
Berries: Using same brush paint berries deep red.

2. Swan
Palette

Base coat: White
Commas: Green
Beak: Red
Eye: Black

Painting guide

Circle: Paint solid gold using #4 brush.
Commas: With #00 brush paint dark green.
Beak: Paint solid red using #2 brush.
Eye: Solid black using #00 brush.

3. Bells
Palette

Base coat: Yellow
Commas: Deep green
Bow: Red
Circle: Silver
Dots: Silver

Painting guide

Bells: Solid yellow using #4 brush.
Commas: Using #00 brush paint deep green.
Bow: Paint deep red using #2 brush.
Circle: Using #4 brush paint silver.
Dots: With #00 brush paint dots silver.

4. Bear
Palette

Base coat: Silver
Stocking: Red + white
Bear: Yellow
Eyes, nose: Black
Parcel: Green + silver

Painting guide

Circle: Paint solid gold using #4 brush.
Stocking: Paint boot red with #4 brush. Paint the fluff on top white using same brush.
Bear: Using #2 brush paint yellow.
Eyes, nose: With #00 brush paint solid black.
Parcel: Using #2 brush paint deep green. Add silver lines and dots with #00 brush.

5. Candle
Palette

Circle: Gold
Candle: Red + black
Flame: Yellow + red

Painting guide

Circle: Paint gold using #4 brush.
Candle: Using #2 brush paint red. Dots paint black using #00 brush.
Flame: With #2 brush paint solid yellow. Then add red in centre with same brush.

6. Sleigh
Palette

Base coat: Gold
Commas, dots: Deep green

Painting guide

Commas, dots: Paint commas using #2 brush. Dots paint deep green using #00 brush.

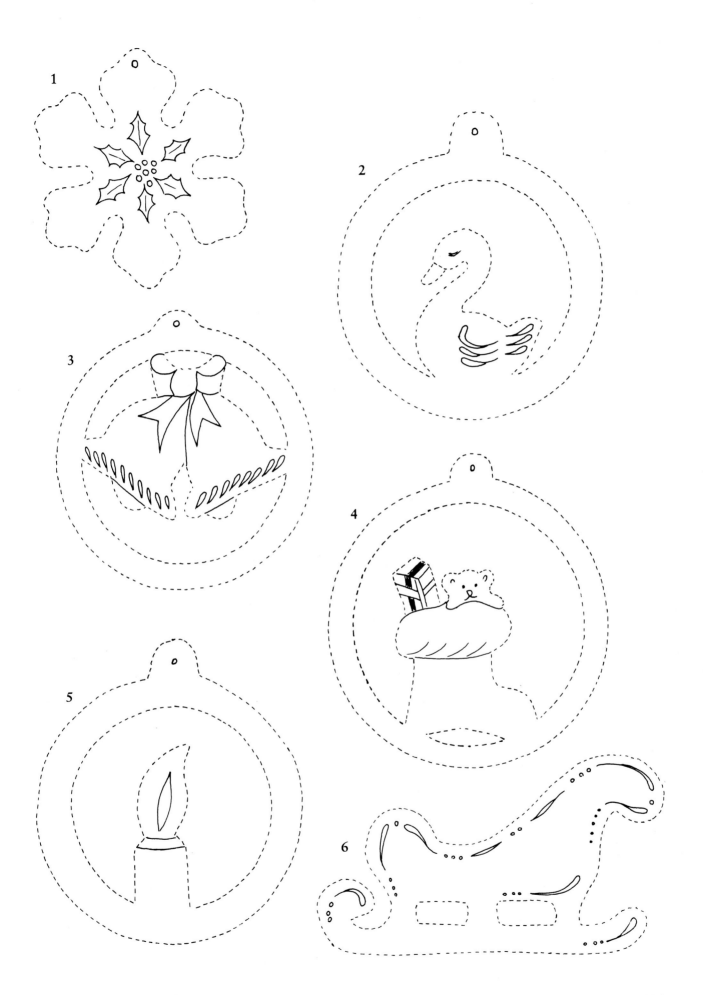

Christmas tree decorations

Illustrated on page 104

Materials

Small wooden Christmas shapes
Paints: Waterbased acrylics
Brushes: #2, #00 round brushes; 12 mm and 25 mm
(½" and 1") flat brushes
Tracing paper, white transfer paper
Varnish: Polyurethane gloss finish
Pencils: 2B and 5H
Sandpaper: Wet-and-dry #400 or #600

Palette

Base coat: Bright red
All details: Gold

Preparation

1. Apply 1 coat of base coat colour to the shapes with 12 mm (½") flat brush.
2. Let dry. Sand lightly, apply second coat of base coat colour. Let dry.
3. Trace design onto tracing paper.
4. Place pattern onto article, slide the white transfer paper between tracing paper and shape.
5. Retrace design with 5H pencil.

Painting guide

Paint all details gold with either #2 or #00 round brush.

Finish

Apply 1 coat of gloss finish polyurethane varnish with 25 mm (1") flat brush. Let dry. Apply a second coat of varnish.

*Large Christmas decorations
and Christmas tree decorations*
(see pages 102 and 105)

Christmas gifts and decorations
(see page 109)

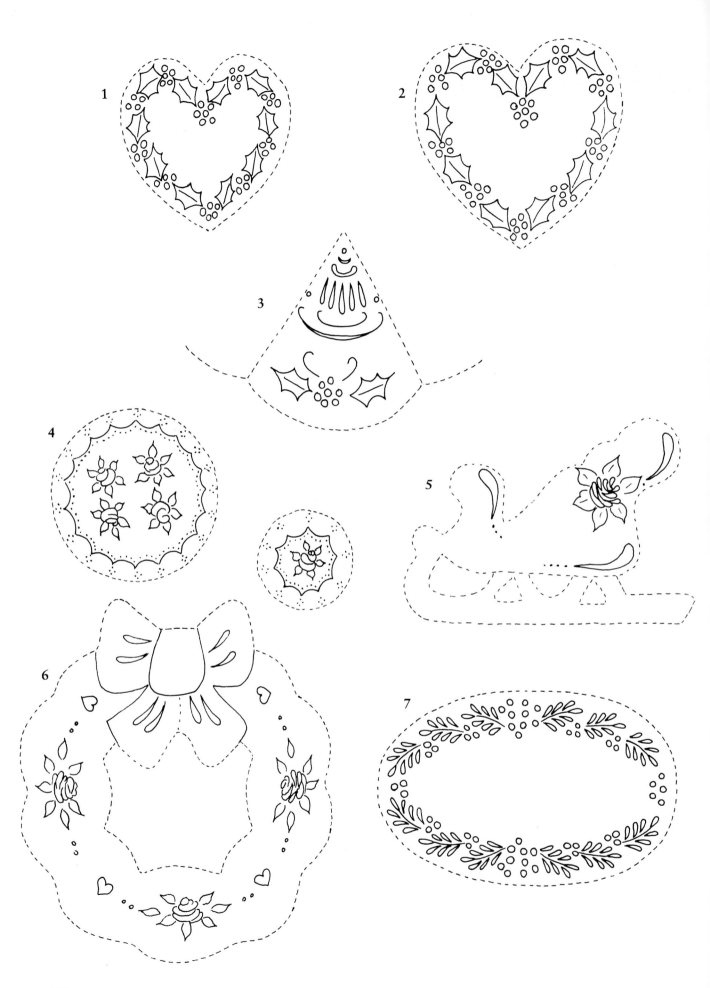

Christmas gifts and decorations

Illustrated on page 107

Follow the general procedures outlined on previous pages for materials and preparation.

1 & 2. Gold and silver boxes
Palette

Base coat: Gold + silver
Leaves: Green
Berries: Red

Painting guide

Leaves: Using #2 brush paint leaves solid green.
Berries: Paint solid red using #00 brush.
For decoration you can add some velvet ribbon around top and base of box.

3. Coaster
Palette

Base coat: Deep green
Berries: Red
Leaves: Gold
Scrolls: Gold

Painting guide

Berries: Using #00 brush paint berries red.
Leaves: With #2 brush paint leaves solid gold.
Scrolls: Paint gold using #00 brush.

4. Earrings and brooch
Palette

Base coat: Black
Leaves: Green + white
Roses: Pink + white
Dots: Gold + white

Painting guide

Leaves: Double load green and white using #00 brush.
Roses: With #00 brush paint roses double loading pink and white.
Dots, scroll: Paint white using #00 brush for all dots. Paint gold scrolls using same brush.

5. Sleigh
Palette

Base coat: Burgundy + gold
Leaves: Gold
Roses: Burgundy + white
Commas: Gold

Painting guide

Leaves: Paint solid gold using #2 brush.
Roses: Double load burgundy and white using #2 brush.
Commas: Paint gold using #2 brush.

6. Wreath
Palette

Base coat: Green
Leaves, rose: Gold
Hearts: Red
Commas: Gold

Painting guide

Leaves, rose: Using #2 brush paint leaves and rose solid gold.
Hearts: Paint red using #2 brush. Outline in gold dots using #00 brush.
Bow: Using #4 brush paint bow red.
Commas: Using #2 brush paint commas in bow gold. For small gold circles use #00 brush.

7. Soap
Palette

Leaves: Green
Berries: Red

Painting guide

Leaves: Using #00 brush paint leaves solid green.
Berries: Paint red with #00 brush.

Easter eggs

Illustrated on back cover

Materials

Assortment of wooden eggs in different sizes
Paints: Waterbased acrylics
Brushes: #2, #00 round brushes; 12 mm and 25 mm (½" and 1") flat brushes
Tracing paper, white transfer paper
Varnish: Polyurethane gloss finish
Pencils: 2B and 5H
Sandpaper: Wet-and-dry #400 or #600

Egg 1

Base coat: White
Leaves: Paint solid green with #2 brush.
Flower petals: With #2 brush paint the petals solid yellow and red.
Centre: Green and white with #2 brush.
Curlicues: Paint red using #00 brush.
Dots: Paint green and red using #00 brush.

Egg 2

Base coat: White
Leaves: Paint dark green with #2 brush.
Flower: Centre is solid red, then add the yellow dots using #2 brush.
Petals: Using #2 brush paint solid bright blue.

Egg 3

Base coat: Mid blue
Leaves: Double load green and white using #2 brush.
Daisies: Double load blue and white using same brush.
Centre paint yellow and white add a touch of brown.
Spray: Paint white using #00 brush.

Egg 4

Base coat: Bright blue
Leaves: Paint green with #2 brush.
Forget-me-nots: Double load blue and white with #00 brush. Centre is yellow.
Daisy: Using #2 brush double load mauve and white.
Tulips: Double load yellow and white using #2 brush.
Dots: With #00 brush paint blue and white.

Egg 5

Base coat: Turquoise
Hearts: Paint solid gold using #2 brush.
Dots: Also gold using same brush. Paint all over egg.

Egg 6

Base coat: Red
Sides: Gold commas using #00 brush.
Dots: Double load gold and white using same brush.
Leaves: Paint solid green using #00 brush.
Flowers: White and yellow dots using #00 brush.
Bunny: Double load light brown and white with #2 brush.
Bow: Solid blue using #00 brush.
Whiskers: Black using same brush.

Egg 7

Base coat: Burgundy
Thin line: Paint gold using #2 brush.
Wider petal: Turquoise using same brush.
Dots: Double load turquoise and gold using #00 brush.
Side pattern: Commas gold using #00 brush.
Dots: Solid turquoise using same brush. Paint same pattern on both sides of egg.

Finish

Apply 2–3 coats of gloss finish polyurethane varnish with 25 mm (1") flat brush.

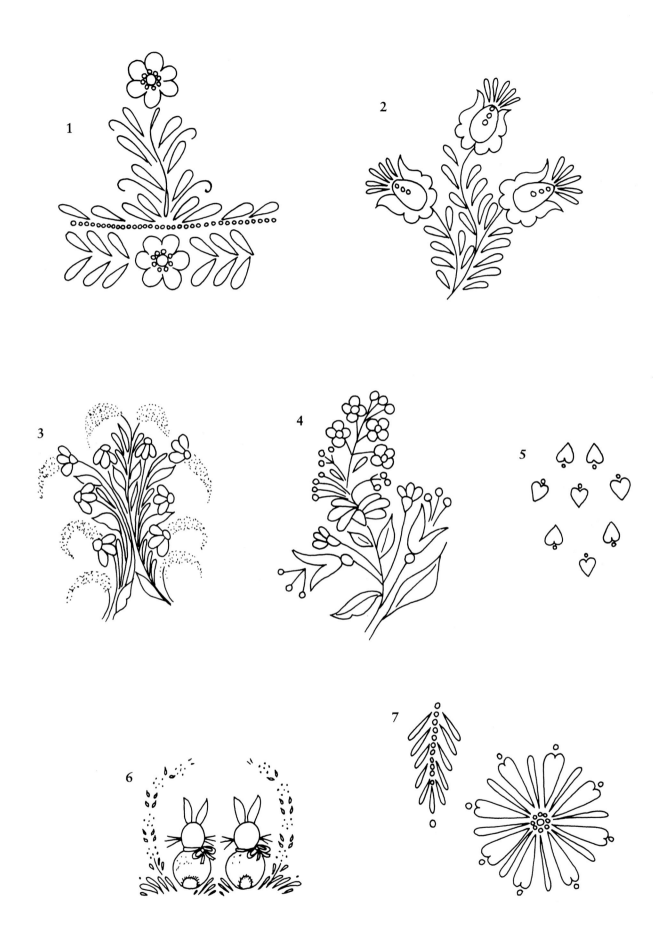

Suppliers

Apart from a few special items which were made for us by a local craftsman, all the articles used in this book were purchased from these suppliers:

Terracotta articles

Terracotta Collectibles
Ian Ward
3 Sorensen Rd
Gympie Qld 4570
(07) 54 82 5205

Wooden articles

Timberturn Pty Ltd
1 Shepley Ave
Panorama SA 5041
(08) 8277 5056

Other folk art titles from Kangaroo Press
by Eva & Nicole Tummel

FOLK ART WITH AUSTRALIAN FLOWERS Eva Tummel
FOLK ART ON TERRACOTTA Eva Tummel
FOLK ART FLOWERS: STEP-BY-STEP Eva Tummel
AUSTRALIAN FOLK ART TREASURES Eva & Nicole Tummel
TRADITIONAL HUNGARIAN FOLK ART Eva & Nicole Tummel
BAUERNMALEREI: FOLK ART FROM EUROPE Eva & Nicole Tummel